THE GROCERY BAG
AND OTHER HAWAIIAN
PARABLES

God bless you
as you seek His will

Ken Smith 5/13/08

THE GROCERY BAG AND OTHER HAWAIIAN PARABLES

Kenneth W. Smith

iUniverse, Inc.
New York Lincoln Shanghai

THE GROCERY BAG AND OTHER HAWAIIAN PARABLES

iUniverse books may be ordered through booksellers or by contacting:

iUniverse
2021 Pine Lake Road, Suite 100
Lincoln, NE 68512
www.iuniverse.com
1-800-Authors (1-800-288-4677)

ISBN-13: 978-0-595-37635-3 (pbk)
ISBN-13: 978-0-595-82026-9 (ebk)
ISBN-10: 0-595-37635-5 (pbk)
ISBN-10: 0-595-82026-3 (ebk)

Printed in the United States of America

Welcome to Hawaii, via <u>The Grocery Bag and other Hawaiian Parables.</u> Hundreds of thousands of people come to the island state. Some come on honeymoons to lie on the warm beach and dream of the rest of their life. Many come for the excitement of Waikiki and the hundreds of shops and eating establishments. Some come to take the flight-seeing trip and must admit Hawai'i from the air looks pretty much the same except for some waterfalls, some beaches and azure water and of course the lava on the Big Island. Some come to take the cruise and get off at the various ports to say they have seen the entire State of Hawai'i.

Some folk come to participate in a convention and they spend every free moment and break out wandering the streets to soak in the atmosphere. Some come to the state for athletic competitions, surfing, football, basketball, soccer and regardless of whether or not they win, they have won the opportunity to visit Hawai'i. Some students come for educational opportunities to study in an atmosphere where snow does not hinder their education.

You have come through this book to see people and to participate in culture and other home town activities. In each case there is an emphasis in the spiritual life of the individual. Welcome, this book is dedicated to you.

I express my appreciation to those who have made the book possible. Many are subjects of the various parables. Helen is an excellent proof reader and Melba does a wonderful job with the illustrations, reading each parable carefully to catch the essence for her art work. The U. S. Postal Service along with Janet Smith were responsible for the cover art and Dick and Judy are ever so helpful in the final product.

In reading this book you have become involved in more than warm beaches, waterfalls and shopping areas. You have become involved in the people, and even the 'critters' that are all around you, the essence of the state. No people on earth hold the 'aina, the land, in greater reverence than do the Hawaiian people. There is not much of it and what there is faces crowding by those who have the wealth to buy pieces of it.

Taking care of what we have becomes very important. The title parable along with many others will show the real aloha, the love of the people as well as of the land. May you carry that love and concern to your own "hive" that the honey of Hawai'i might fill the rest of the country.

Contents

INTRODUCTION

Jesus came to earth at just the right time. There was a Roman peace, Pax Romana, that was enforced by the military might of Rome. There was good communication and transportation created by the Romans. They needed to send troops to the foreign provinces in order to maintain order among the conquered people. The bounty, or taxes collected, had to be safely transported to Rome.

The concept of one God had been pushed throughout the then known world by the removal of God's people from Jerusalem. Everywhere a Hebrew family went, the concept of one God also went. In their private worship, in their dealings with others, the concept was always present.

But there were difficulties that Jesus faced. There were four popular languages in vogue at the time. Greek especially the language of literature and philosophy was one of these four. It was a very accurate language. When one wrote in Greek, specific data could be conveyed without confusion of meaning. When it came to recording Christ's words and thoughts for the future, the accuracy of the Greek language was brought into play. It was also true that at times it was necessary to coin new words, but always the meaning of the Greek words used sufficed to make the new meaning.

Aramaic was the local language of the Jewish folk. It was a vernacular used by Jewish folk from all the regions that they occupied. That meant that family that had been separated by the dispersion could still communicate with each other when they gathered together during sacred worship times.

Hebrew was the worship language, the language of the sacred scriptures and the language that contained the Hebrew History, Law, Psalms, Proverbs and the Prophets. It was the only language spoken in the temple area and, as religion played a very important part in the life of a Hebrew family, it was necessary that everyone in the family know the language.

Latin, the language of the Roman occupier, became the official language for deeds and other legal documents. Though some legal documents might be written in Hebrew, to be truly official they had to be translated into Latin. The Roman occupiers were very accepting of the Jewish folk and their faith, even to not directly occupying Jerusalem except at times of special worship and celebration, when riots might occur.

1

Jesus then faced the problem of teaching in such a way that regardless of what language or thought form he used, his teachings might be understood and remembered. He took it for granted that the leaders of the Hebrew nation understood Hebrew and were skilled in remembering the law, the prophets and the lives of the saints that had been recorded in the Old Testament, the only scriptures of the day.

It is recorded in Matthew 13:34,35 that "Jesus spoke all these things to the crowd in parables; he did not say anything to them without using a parable. So was fulfilled what was spoken through the prophet: 'I will open my mouth in parables, I will utter things hidden since the creation of the world.'"

This prophet was the writer of Psalm 78. The first four verses read, "O my people, hear my teaching; listen to the words of my mouth; I will open my mouth in parables, I will utter hidden things, things from of old—what we have heard and known, what our fathers have told us. We will not hide them from their children; we will tell the next generation the praiseworthy deeds of the Lord, his power, and the wonders he has done."

There then follow sixty-eight verses where the Psalmist explains all the wonderful things that God has done. He gives a brief history of God's people and then reminds them of all the things that God has provided for them, in spite of how they treated him. This Psalm could be the basis for a year of sermons without repetition.

The parables in this book are all situated in Hawai'i. Hopefully there is spiritual wisdom in the recounting of the various incidents. Of course when the author talks to birds, insects or fish in some situations the conversations are his own, though for the most part the animal, bird, insect or fish was there. In some cases he uses the actual names of persons, with permission, and in other cases he uses an alias, either because the person is deceased or because he has not been able to contact the person for permission.

Hopefully you can read the parables and gain an insight into the many varied cultures found on the island chain. If there are errors in the text the author can claim them as his own. After thirty-one years of contact he is still learning when it comes to living in the Island State, so occasionally there has to be a readjustment in order to be totally accurate. He admits that the author's theology has crept into the book, but asks that you consider it as you determine your own theological approach to life. He appreciates all those, too numerous to mention, who have assisted in the writing of this book.

I know a good God, who has done a wonderful job in creating, not only the world in which we live, but also the persons who people this world. It is my hope that you can realize how wonderful he is, not only here in creation, but also in salvation for the future. It is my hope that all might come to know him and live together here in peace, and together in the future in his nearer presence. Certainly, Jesus Christ has done his part, and the Holy Spirit keeps working through us. May God bless each of you. Ken Smith

THE EYE

"Be still and know that I am God; I will be exalted among the nations, I will be exalted in the earth."

—Psalm 46:10

The wind had been building up for hours. The radio and television stations were on emergency alert, emphasizing time after time the probable force of the wind and the effects of the soon-to-be-upon-us storm. It was really not that necessary; we had been through our own hurricane and did not need another to experience the terror of the wind.

The stores were full of shoppers anticipating the needs for the next few days, water, candles, canned food and more water. The cars formed a line at the stations that still had gasoline for when the full blast of the storm hit all power would be off and no gas would be available. Animals were brought into shelter, some windows were boarded up and when the siren went off the community was almost prepared for the storm.

Most in the community had been through several storms and though a few were proud enough to try to stay with their homes, most realized that survival statistics proved you were wise to get to a shelter. Later you could take care of what was left of your home.

Glancing out a window, we saw a piece of metal roofing lifted up into the air and sent on its slicing way, going through the branches of a tree and coming to rest at a half-cut hedge, only to be flipped over by the wind and sent on its spinning way into the neighbor's yard. Another piece of metal roofing flew to the top of a neighboring tree and there it would lodge for years, as no one seemed to want to retrieve it.

It was time to abandon what had once been considered a permanent dwelling and head for shelter. The intensity of the wind increased so that the roar could not be identified as coming from anywhere or going anywhere, but just as a constant existence. The airlines had moved their planes to other islands as soon as they knew where the storm would be at its worst. Those tourists who could get out had gone and others were secured in safe places in the hotels. (They were going to get something extra for their money, something that they would long remember.

The travel brochures never seemed to mention that with luck you might experience a real live hurricane in paradise, that paradise was not always that heavenly. Hopefully they had read information on the first few pages of the telephone book, that informed you of what to expect when the wind came, and possibly after.)

It seemed as though everyone and everything had found a place of shelter. It had been forecast when and where the eye of the storm would be passing. It seemed that it would be directly over us. With the early detection system they were almost always correct. The success of the system was to have zero fatalities by the time the storm had passed. Meanwhile, leaves were shredded from the trees and plastered the outside walls of buildings as the intensity increased. Homes along the shore were all abandoned as waves pounded the docks and other buildings. A wave lifted a Volkswagen 'bug' and carried it eight hundred feet into a cane field; where it would stay until the storm was over and then would be driven out of the field.

Then the eye of the storm approached, always a difficult time as the wind, which had been consistently blowing in one direction, after the eye passed, blew from the entirely opposite direction.

Finally there was silence. One could almost call it a dead silence but the trees that lost their branches, were still alive and would grow first small branches and then larger and longer branches to show that there was life after the storm. Buildings that looked dead would be repaired, roof girders strengthened and life would go on, but for now there was silence.

This happened to be a daylight hurricane so as we stepped out we could look up into the eye of the storm, indeed an eerie feeling. There, in huge swarms, were the sea birds that had no place to hide. Instead of fleeing, they gathered in the eye and were smoothly sailing along with the storm. Destruction was before them and destruction was after them, but they were in the quiet of the eye. It seemed that there were millions of them riding out the storm in the eye. When the intensity dropped, which would happen soon, they would resume their relationship with the sea.

Most of us experience the storms of life and many may even dread the experience. It might be a loss of job, a painful loss when one is far advanced in his or her job career, or a possibility of a move, from a location that was thought to be permanent. The storm might be the death of a loved one or possibly the impending death of ones self. Though the storm may seem paltry and insignificant to others, the storm is always of great consequence to the one who experiences it.

Then we should be aware of the sea birds that have not escaped from the storms that they must experience; but, have headed to the center of the trouble and there, there is quiet. Is it any wonder that the psalmist expressed the feeling that when things are howling all around you move to the eye of the storm where God is, and the still small voice is sufficient to all who would hear?

The experienced individual recognizes that we are not going to quiet the storm, we are merely going to be quiet in it. God never promised that he would keep all storms from your life, and to think that he did is to show your faith's infancy. God did not give us the opportunity to always escape the calamity but rather the ability to move to the eye and experience the still, small but very audible, word of God.

"Gracious God, we all have our own storms, storms that we may have brought on ourselves, or just experienced as an 'act of God.' In such times may we have the ability to face the storm and acknowledge the tremendous power that you show, but at the same time move to the center and listen for your still, small, but very real, voice. In your son's name we pray. Amen"

GLADYS

"I am the good shepherd; I know my sheep and my sheep know me—just as the Father knows me and I know the Father—and I lay down my life for the sheep. I have other sheep that are not of this sheep pen. I must bring them also. They too will listen to my voice, and there shall be one flock and one shepherd."

—John 10:14–16

Gladys, of course, was not her name, but Gladys is now her name. She was born in Lilampur, many miles up the Ganges River in India. The family had been looking for, and for nine months waited for, a boy, but she wasn't, she was a girl. Most of the girls in the village were put out to die at the garbage dump at the end of the village. What was needed was a son who would carry on the name and the work, on the property that the family owned, small though it was. It was adjacent to the great River Ganges that controlled all of life.

When she was old enough she joined others in the fields, doing the plowing with the leather straps that were connected to the plow across her shoulders. When it came time to sow, she was good at sowing the grain and could distribute more seed than any of her brothers. When the farming was finished for a season, she joined still others in the adjacent woods gathering small pieces of wood that would be used for fuel in the family cooking fire. She was happy doing no studying except for an awareness of the religious sentiments of the community, they being Hindu.

When she was eligible, which was determined by the need to be put out of the family or to be made available to be a wife to some man, she was married and with her husband farmed a piece of land, adjacent to her home and his home and of course adjacent to the Ganges that controlled their lives.

The river also controlled other things: their drinking and washing, the fertilization of their fields, the transportation to Gaalumpur, the only major city anywhere around. During the monsoon season the rains came in unbelievable torrents and the river rose. The river now took their land, and their home and ultimately, the river took the life of Gladys.

Gladys was merely one of many who likewise lost their lives in the raging torrent of the stream. Because she was not wanted to begin with, and was an insignificant part of the village with no offspring, few missed her as her body floated and bloated down the Ganges. Closer to the ocean, where the tide water backed up the Ganges, her body rested on the banks of the river. There it lay, with thousands of other bodies until all the flesh was gone and only the bones continued to stand out as a white beacon in a sea of drying mud.

Some Americans were in the large city intent on gathering many skeletons to be sold for scientific purposes in their homeland. Now Gladys became very important, for almost all of her bones were in one place. Though a nonentity before, she was now very important. Carefully she was gathered and placed in a burlap bag and the gathering individual was glad to get baksheesh for his labor.

Gladys now traveled thousands of miles from her home town, and her home river. She ultimately was placed in a science laboratory in a small high school in the almost Western-most town on the Island of Kaua'i, in the United States of America. She had no immigration papers, there was no physical examination to determine that she was not carrying diseases, she was just a pile of bones, given the name Gladys, (not necessarily appreciated by anyone whose name happened to be Gladys).

There, in the high school laboratory, with hundreds of little wires holding her bones in place, hundreds of students knew her as the skeleton that they used to learn about the human body. They felt her ribs, her femur, her hips, her spinal cord, her skull, her fingers and her toes. Though before no one paid any attention to her at all, now students paid intense attention as they were tested about her bones. and she was very important.

For years Gladys hung in the science laboratory where she was known to thousands of students who have since their high school days carried their knowledge of Gladys all over the world. Finally plastics and computer chips won out and

Gladys was no longer needed. However, Gladys was a person at one time and still had the bones to prove it. She was not to be thrown out as any other bit of clutter when mandated by the need for more space. The official school personnel and students decided that Gladys should be buried. A plot was donated by a neighboring Christian church and Gladys, with a full Christian funeral service but no eulogy, became the only Hindu buried in the Christian cemetery.

She has now passed again into the anonymity of advancing time where all those who carry markers that identify them and their relationships, are together. There is now a marker planned for Gladys even though no one really knows her history. God, to whom Gladys has always been a real person, has a place of rest for her in his presence.

"Loving heavenly Father, though many know you as the maker of rules, and others know you as a tyrant who mandates that your will only should be done, we recognize that you are a loving heavenly father, who loves each person ever born on the planet earth. Bless Gladys, and all the other non-entities, and even us. May we regard no person as lesser than we ourselves, for all are loved by you. In your son's name we pray. Amen."

THE LAST SUPPER OR THE
INVISIBLE PATRONS

"Just then a woman who had been subject to bleeding for twelve years came up behind him and touched the edge of his cloak. She said to herself, 'If I only touch his cloak, I will be healed.' Jesus turned and saw her. 'Take heart, daughter,' he said, 'your faith has healed you.' And the woman was healed from that moment."

—Matthew 9:20–22

It had been five years since we had been together and to mark the very special occasion we decided to eat out at a local restaurant. It was to be a celebratory meal in honor of one person's birthday.

Arriving at the restaurant we were ushered by the maitre 'd to a table immediately adjacent to the kitchen, particularly that part of the kitchen that contained the dish washer and also the ice crusher. As two of our party had hearing aids and the ice crusher sounded like an eighteen-wheel truck passing over the table, we asked to be seated a little further from the kitchen.

The maitre 'd was very kind in setting up a table for the five of us, though there were many other tables that were already set up for the evening meal. Once the table was ready we were escorted to it, given our ice water and menus, and then left alone. This table was not in an isolated corner but more or less in the middle of those tables being served. Within minutes we had determined our individual orders and placed the menus in a place to indicate that we were ready to order.

And so we waited and waited and waited. Several other couples and families arrived at the restaurant, were seated, their orders taken and they advanced to the salad bar. Then many other couples arrived, were seated, placed their orders and advanced to the salad bar. The nearest waiter and waitress passed our table many times, but we could not arouse their interest in us. Time passed. The waiter and waitress paused for long conversations at neighboring tables, but every time they passed our table, they seemed to look straight ahead. The thought did come to me that I might trip one of them and then they would see us, but I put it out of my mind.

Finally they began taking a devious route from the tables that they served so that they did not pass by ours. Occasionally we would lift our menus but still they did not see us. By this time we had to consult the menus again as we had forgotten what our orders were going to be.

First there were feelings of embarrassment that we were being passed by; we were guests and we had special guests. Then it almost became anger. After forty-five minutes our only discussion became how to leave the restaurant without making a scene. We needn't have worried. They did not even see us. No one looked in our direction; it was as though we were invisible.

We tried to analyze what had gone wrong. We had patronized the restaurant for over thirty years, since before any of the waiters or waitresses had been born. We were dressed like everyone else in the restaurant. We had greeted the maitre 'd warmly, using a local greeting rather than a tourist greeting. Possibly their inattention to us was due to the fact that they set up a special table but it was really not necessary as several tables were never used, though they had been set up for patrons.

We could have advanced to the salad bar but the procedure followed by everyone else in the restaurant was to first have your order taken and then move to the salad bar. We had no food so we couldn't demonstrate that our table manners were good or bad. We were not boisterous, though there were others in the restaurant who were. The waiters and waitresses were not pushed for busyness as they spent time with other parties or families in long conversation and then they would retreat to the kitchen which seemed to be a haven for them. We really didn't feel that we should beg to be waited on, though it almost came to that. Finally, to save further embarrassment for us, we just eased out silently into the darkened parking area found our car and departed.

We then went to another restaurant, one we had never visited, in the same community. It had been over an hour since we had planned on eating, and we were more than hungry. There was only one waitress serving all of the patrons, but we were seated, received personal greetings, water and menus and also suggestions about the specials. The minute we laid down the menus, the waitress was there, took our order and mentioned that because of one entree ordered, the preparation would be a little longer than usual. She took a personal responsibility to make sure that our water glasses were kept full, a sign of an excellent waiter or waitress.

She again returned and mentioned that the meals were almost ready. Her personality was more pleasant than any of the personalities of the waiters and waitresses of the first restaurant! She was a delight and we proved it when we added the tip. That one waitress saved the evening and gave a sugary ending to what could have been a bitter dining out experience.

Then I thought of a recent experience in a local church. How many individuals attended either for the first time or for several times, and were only greeted at the door and shown a seat? Normally that seat was in the center section of a row. All around regular attenders were greeting their friends and family members, getting settled for the worship service, checking the bulletin, providing coloring materials to the children and sort of 'settling in'.

Meanwhile one individual read the church bulletin (menu) to see what was going to happen that morning. If there were asterisks then she knew when to stand. She noted that the hymns were going to be familiar and looked forward to the various parts of the service.

Meanwhile people had been ushered to the same pew and they sat at either the right end or the left end. They did not dream of entering the sanctity of the single person sitting in the middle. No one turned around to greet the stranger; no one leaned forward to greet the stranger, so the stranger remained a stranger. The stranger did serve a purpose though: when it came time for the offering, she got up to receive the collection plate on the right-hand side of the pew and passed it to the folks on the left-hand end of the pew. It was good that she was there.

When the service ended folks spent time catching up on all the news that they missed before the service began. She knew no one and though she nodded, the nods were merely acknowledged and people turned away. The pastor greeted her warmly at the door, his handshake was real but then she was out the door and on her own. She passed several individuals and couples in the parking lot but they were all single-mindedly on their way to their cars, church now being over.

Is there a lesson in our being invisible patrons? I hope so. We have spent time just trying to find the main entrance to sanctuaries, that really were not sanctuaries. We have been those lonely folk sitting in the middle of empty pews, passing the offering baskets. We have stood in line to shake the pastor's hand and been ignored by all around.

Now let me add a reassurance. A friend went through a devastating divorce, where it seemed that she and everything that she stood for was rejected and crushed. In desperation, the week following the divorce she sought out refuge in a nearby church, only two blocks from where she lived that she had never entered in her many years of marriage. She always knew that it was there, but she had never needed it and had no inclination to attend any of its meetings. She was greeted at the door, shown to a pew next to a gracious couple who explained the order of worship. She remembered the hymns from her days of youth, was involved in warm conversation, and the pastor 'sought her out' on her way past him at the door after the service. She felt ministered to for the first time in the three years of the crumbling marriage relationship.

To Christ every individual was, and is, a very real person who was, and is, to be treated that way. No one was ignored by Jesus or even some of his followers, even though some came not to serve or be served but rather to argue and religiously pout. As Christ's representative to each and every individual with whom you come in contact, what kind of a waiter or waitress are you?

"Gracious father, we hope to remember that we are all part of your family and no one of us is to be ignored. Yes, we come to worship you but we come also seeking fellowship with others, be they children or ancients. Help us to be a warm and truly loving family, truly interested in all around us, because we are interested in you and all who are yours. This we pray in your son's name. Amen."

KJW 234

"I am the Lord your God...You shall have no other gods before me...You shall not make for yourself an idol...You shall not misuse the name of the Lord your God...Remember the Sabbath day by keeping it holy...Honor your father and your mother...You shall not murder...You shall not commit adultery...You shall not steal...You shall not give false testimony...You shall not covet anything of your neighbor." Spiritual rules of the road of life.

—Exodus 20:1–17.

Well, KJW 234 we had quite a ride today, didn't we. We were behind you for over 18 miles, but not because we didn't try to get ahead of you. We slowed down when you slowed down and, with a chance to pass safely, we tried. But you thwarted us, didn't you? Did you know that when you drive with your hand dangling out of the window, it is a sign that you are going to slow down and stop?

Did you know when you put your hand straight out to the left, it is a sign that you are going to turn left? (Though of course there was no side street on which you could have turned and then you put your hand up as though you were going to turn right.) Of course you didn't bother using your directional signals, because you really did not want to turn at all.

Also, did you realize that today you drove anywhere between the speed limit and fifteen miles per hour below the speed limit, though there were many cars behind you, at one time a procession of nine? Did you realize that every time you turned to talk with your girlfriend or your wife that you drove to the right and often crossed over the sideline marker of the lane? It was also interesting that when you stopped in that small town for the red light that you stopped about ten car lengths from the car in front of you.

At first I though that possibly you were trying to get personal but then I realized that your arm out of the window was just a nonchalance that you wished to show. Of course you have driven that road hundreds of times and I hope with a little more diligence than you showed today.

There was one chance to pass you, you know where there are two lanes of traffic on the hill and of course you got the race-horse syndrome because on that stretch, when I tried to pass you, you were finally going 65 miles per hour, which is way too fast for that lane of highway, so I backed off. It was not that I was not challenged because we had seen much of the back of your car, so much so that I memorized your tag number.

Then I realized that you were just driving the way you normally drive. After we both turned off the highway you continued to frustrate all of us who were behind you. You did an excellent job of controlling traffic though that probably was not your intent. So we all backed off and finally when we got to the town that we had chosen, you went a different way, but I imagined that you looked back to see which way I was going to turn before you made your decision

It is my hope that when you drive on the mainland that you heed the good driving rules that are enforced by the police. If it is necessary to completely turn your head and body to face the person who is riding with you I would suggest that she snuggle up to you so that you can hear her and she can hear you. Or else it might be wise to get a hearing device. It is disconcerting to those driving behind you when you don't stay in your lane and at a normal consistent speed, to say nothing of those who prefer not to have a head on collision with you.

If you are really bored, please let someone else drive. Bored or not, a head on collision at 50 miles per hour can be a 100 mile an hour smash with an oncoming car.

Well, you got to the town ahead of us, by at least a second and a half. And you taught us to be virtuous, because patience is virtuous. I don't know how the other drivers who were behind you felt, because we turned off. I would not want to have stopped you as from your driving habits you do not seem like a nice person, and I prefer to share the highway with nice people, who all follow all the same rules. I find that some do not, and must suffer for it, or their relatives suffer for their loss. Might I suggest, "Happy Driving."

"Gracious God, help us to be considerate of others, seeking to show in our habits, including driving, that we are aware of all those who are around us. We thank you for the Ten Commandments. Help us to put them into such practice that they automatically become part of our lifestyle. In Christ's name we pray. Amen"

THE BEE

"You will all fall away," Jesus told them, "for it is written: 'I will strike the shepherd, and the sheep will be scattered.' But after I have risen, I will go ahead of you into Galilee.' Peter declared, 'even if all fall away, I will not.' 'I tell you the truth,' Jesus answered, 'tomorrow-yes, tonight-before the rooster crows twice you yourself will disown me three times.' But Peter insisted emphatically, 'Even if I have to die with you, I will never disown you.' And all the others said the same."

—Mark 14:27–31

The Royal Poinciana tree was beautiful. The root spread of the tree was just about as wide as its height. The roots dominated the yard; they would crawl along under the accompanying grass and come to the surface only to again head down into the turf.

When the flowers came into blossom the tree became a gorgeous orange decoration that enhanced the entire yard. There wasn't the magnificent cloud of scent surrounding the tree, as is often found in Hawai'i, but the bees were attracted. To sit under the tree was to enjoy the hum of hundreds of bees that had been attracted to the tree and that carried the pollen to accompanying trees and also to the hives located on the edge of the cliff.

Almost all the bees were the honeybees, though at times wasps could be seen enjoying the spread that the tree gave for all visitors. There was another bee that should have been a warning but it also was enjoying the blossoms, yet it lingered. It did not move off to other trees, nor was there a hive that could be seen. In a sense it was a lone bee, but it was also a signal. It was a part of a group of eight bees, all black except for one that was tan. It was a carpenter bee.

Carpenter bees are not interested in hives, like other bees, but in wood that is dead. And this bee lingered. Of no concern to the other bees, at least at the present, this bee was aware that the nutrients that flowed up the trunk of the tree, protected only by the bark, were supporting a dying tree.

The tree had been alive to many bees and also to many others. Children had hung a swing from one of its large branches and had spent hours swinging back and forth, protected from the rain by the leaves overhead. Others had stretched a hammock and spent hours resting in the warmth of Hawaiian afternoons.

But there was still more. The tree was involved in history of sorts. Folks who had lived their entire lives in the local community claimed that they had seen menehunes, little workers of a past Hawai'i, jumping from one branch to another and when discovered, retreating to the basement of an adjoining home. (The people were the students and teachers of a neighboring school. The tree would always be remembered for its historical relationship.)

The tree was soon to pass into history, for the next few years were dry years. The roots, in true Royal Poinciana style, had traveled to find sustenance in many directions and not always under-ground. They could be seen crawling along the top of the ground until they found nutrients and then would dig deep again. This made it difficult for those who mowed the lawn as the mower would hang up on the elevated roots.

Finally the tree came to the end of its life. No longer could it support the branches, leaves or blossoms. The center of the tree had rotted away and the carpenter bees enjoyed their home and the honey bees found their pollen in other places. So it was decided to cut the tree down and a long work session ensued that ended the life of the tree and left only a large stump about four feet high, and about three feet wide.

An advertisement for wood brought only one inquiry. They wanted the wood, but they wanted it in stove-length size, split for immediate usage and delivered–even stacked–in a camping area in an adjacent mountainous area. No volunteers could be found to perform such an exacting wood gathering chore, though the wood would have been valuable. So it was decided to take the chunks that had been cut, to make it more manageable and split them to be burned on the site.

Aha, the bees were still there! To view a cross section of the stump showed that they had enjoyed themselves. (It is easy to pun that they had made holey wood near the house that was owned by the church). They did not kill the tree, they just took advantage of it. When the first wedge was pounded into a block of the tree the carpenter bees swarmed out of their holey home. Had they been the stinging kind of bee, and some claim that they were, the man on the end of the sledge would have been stung. But the bees merely moved to another block of wood and so it continued. They were not angry; they were just determined.

Then it was time to burn the stump. A fire was set on the stump and it burned and burned, some of the fire even following the roots out away from the original fire. Meanwhile, the bees were becoming very disturbed. Time and time again they would swarm and the man on the sledge would back off. When the final chunk of the tree was consumed, the bees all moved off to other trees, except for one lone carpenter bee. Long after the huge tree had turned to white ash the lone carpenter bee would buzz into the hole made by the burned stump.

The other black bees and the lone tan bee have since disappeared, but the one carpenter bee is still in the neighborhood. Just a few minutes ago he was seen again, flying round and round, where the stump used to be.

There is a loyalty exhibited in that bee that is hard to understand. We who are involved in the church long for that kind of loyalty. Though all things may seem to have changed, and many have decided that there are other places to place their trust, those who are loyal are the ones who bring tears of affection to the eyes.

Peter claimed that loyalty when he realized that Christ was going to be persecuted. The loyalty-love-respect for his master moved him to declare that he would never leave the master. Though he did three times deny his relationship, he stayed the course longer than the other disciples.

Such loyalty is found in our God who is so loyal to us though we often would seemingly turn our backs on his love. He is always willing to forgive and to give us new life. And the question remains, are we loyal to him? Is he the one who is thanked every time something good happens to us? Is he the one who is thanked when the good things happen, and we would seemingly take the credit? Is he thanked for the talents he has given us and for the creativity we show through those talents? Is he thanked for the love of family and friends, for the health that we enjoy, for the happiness that we feel? For, he is the author of all things and to him we owe our total allegiance.

"Gracious God, may I be as loyal to you as that bee still is to his burned out home, the stump. Just a moment ago I visited that burned-out stump and the bee is still there. Yesterday there were wonderful things that happened, and so I thank you. You are so loyal, and your people are, too. Help me to be loyal not only to you but to those whom you have favored me with as family and friends. Help me regularly to show that loyalty and love to you and to yours. In your son's name I pray. Amen."

CYCLES OF HAWAI'I

"I am like an olive tree flourishing in the house of God; I trust in God's unfailing love forever and ever. I will praise you forever for what you have done in your name. I will hope, for your name is good. I will praise you in the presence of your saints.

—Psalm 52:8,9

It was a quiet night at the beach. The lull of the quiet surf did not disturb the conversation but rather enhanced the genuineness of the moment, for with the family gathered, the couple announced that she was pregnant and in seven months there would be a new child in the *ohana*, another chapter in the passages of the family. And:

Again the family was gathered when she gave birth to the sweetest bundle of joy an individual could ever lay eyes upon. *Tutu* was thrilled, grandfather was pleased as Hawaiian Punch, and the nephews and nieces could not wait to spread the good news. "She looks just like Grandma." "No, She has the eyes of Grandpa and the mouth of Grandma." And they each picked a particular part of her body and when they were finished the baby belonged, because every part resembled some part of some person who was already in the *Ohana*. Ah, what a beautiful composite. She was another chapter, and in being born she inherited many aunties and uncles. And:

The child was raised in the warm *aloha* that is openly shown in the life of an Hawaiian family, where every child is wanted, each treated with an extra amount of love, and mysteriously, each gets more than 100% of the love of the family. And then the time came for school, with pads, pencil boxes, a new lunch box, adorned with the cartoon character of the latest fad, just like everyone else's lunch box. But hers was filled with wonderful *aloha* and theirs sometimes seemed a little skimpy. And:

The days passed rapidly through the primary years and the difficult days of junior high, into the senior high years. There was the usual amount of day dreaming when the sky was blue, the room was hot and the surfing waves, the

22

opihi rocks, the outrigger practice canoe in the river all took precedence over the print in the books. A few cautious words from the teacher and the principal brought reality to the child and high school graduation was attained.

They were the same buildings and almost the same teachers, now older than you could ever imagine, teachers who knew your whole family because they had experienced the same troubles with them in the same rooms with the same features of Hawaiian life. Graduation brought out a charm seldom seen before, a dimpled smile that warmed everyone who saw her. She had a clearness of skin, a determined look that had brought excellence to studies, skill to athletics, a host of honest friends who would be such for the rest of her life and a love of the *'aina*, the land of her birth. Added to all of this was the grace of the *hula* that emphasized watching the hands but affected the bearing of the entire person.

To be fully human, fully Hawaiian, fully loved and appreciated, that was what Hawaiian living was all about. High school had rushed past and now, behind her, was graduation, with all the tests passed. With the future planned graduation became a happy blur, even the practice procession. ("What am I doing here already and it seems that I just got started".)

The graduation speaker spoke directly to her, there was the recessional and then she found her alphabetical place on the field and there was the warmth of the family, the *leis* stacked so high that she could scarcely see over them, the affectionate hugs from all the fellow classmates, those with whom she had competed for four years, but whom she loved greatly, and the tremendous pride in her family, her *'ohana*, and hence another chapter in the passages of the family. And:

College brought new endeavor, a host of new friends that would be a new *'ohana* until the time of her death. One of those friends was very special and soon after college graduation there was another marriage, a new home, a new position in the community, new responsibilities but still the *'ohana* was an irreplaceable unit in the community, in time and in eternity.

There is an endlessness in the cycles of Hawai'i. Daily the sun makes it passage across the sky, monthly the moon travels from east to west, annually the stars make their traverse through the heavens but the passages are as narrow as the individual and as wide as the 'ohana.

God has allotted each of us a passage through time. To some it is a trip so short that it seems but a ripple on the surface of humanity, remembered with visits to the graveyard and a brief life span inscribed on a headstone. Always the life is talked of in context of what he or she did with his or her life. There may be a small cross, decorated with plastic flowers, on some curve of the road, or a brief note in the paper telling of the passing, but usually only the 'ohana remembers and the individual's name is given to someone else in the family, a ripple of remembrance.

Others seem to create a tidal wave as thousands are affected by their deep rivers of life but each individual must live the life that is given by God. Though living with many others, we die as individuals. How good it is to have been chosen by God to be part of the cycles of life in Hawai'i.

"God grant us the ability to live our lives in tune with your will. May that which we have done be in your best interest that we might give the most that we have to your honor and Glory. In the name of Jesus, who had his own 'ohana, we pray. Amen."

KEN WAS HERE

"And God said, 'I will be with you. And this will be the sign to you that it is I who have sent you: When you have brought the people out of Egypt, you will worship God on this mountain.' Moses said to God, 'Suppose I go to the Israelites and say to them, The God of your father has sent me to you and they ask me, What is his name? Then what shall I tell them?' God said to Moses, 'I am who I am. This what you are to say to the Israelites; I am has sent me to you.'"

—Exodus 3:12–14

Throughout the geographical world and timeless ages, since mankind has learned to draw, civilization has been plagued with graffiti. The deep urge to express oneself erupts in drawings and expressions displayed over any surface smooth enough to accept chalk, pencil, stone or paint. If there is some other medium, surely it has been used to leave what was hoped to be a lasting message.

During World War II an imaginary person known as Kilroy circled the world, wherever American servicemen went, documenting the fact that he had been there. There was no place, from the jungles of the Pacific, to the battlefields of Europe, to the wastelands of the far north that Kilroy had not visited, not once but many times. Always he left his calling card, "Kilroy was here." In many places tons and tons of concrete were used to build the bulwarks of defense, yet all that remains are the walls with the message, "Kilroy was here."

Now restroom walls seem to bear the brunt of this urge for self expression. There really is no place immune from the plague of the person, bent on self expression in words or pictures. Advice for followers, stories of battles lost and won, warnings of future displays of courage—all are encoded on the walls of just about every conceivable structure. In some cases the artists or writers had to hang upside down, bat-like, to express themselves and then imagine what the message would look like when viewed right side up.

One of the most beautiful graffiti expressions is located under one of the H-l Freeway bridges. Pictures showing hot rod cars and aircraft battles as well as the beauty of Hawaiian beaches, valleys and mountains with waterfalls, are accompanied by the chalk drawing of a heart and the words,"Tawnie and Donn love each other."

Often graffiti expresses the feelings of one person for another, but seldom are there such forms of love as this expression carries. They love each other, which implies that both Tawnie and Donn wrote the expression together.

In order to write this message the artist or artists had to stand in the middle of Nuuanu Stream as it slowly meanders its way to the Honolulu harbor. As a slowly meandering stream is very slippery underfoot some one had to stand on something in order to reach the top of the writing, with the slippery concrete as the base for the wooden box or ladder. It takes little imagination to see the writer one moment about to post the dream phrase and the next moment being drenched in the slimy water.

If you do not know the message is there, you will probably never see it or know that it exists. It is dark in that tunnel. Very few want to trespass over the slimy concrete, and when you are slipping and sliding you rarely look at the walls, but rather where the next foot is going to be placed. Thousands of cars are driving over you, horns are blasting, planes are taking off and city noises abound, but that one silent message possibly says more than all the other noise. This is a message for each other, Tawnie and Donn, and it lasts, whether the rest of the world knows or cares at all.

I don't imagine that Tawnie and Donn will bring their children or grandchildren to that spot though its adjacency to a park might lead to this possibility. I know nothing of Tawnie and Donn except that the message may be washed off the next time that there is a violent rain shower causing a full Nuuanu Stream, and possibly it has been erased by nature as I write. But isn't that how life is? So often we say the words and the intent is carried, but memory of it is lost. Oh, we have been told that somewhere, somehow, man will be able to point a receiver out into space and recover messages that had once been spoken but lost to history. But it could be that only in the memories of the sender and the receiver will the message really be recorded.

We need to remember that God was there, and is here, as an eternal Kilroy. Each sunrise, each sunset, each rainbow, each daylight hour or nighttime vigil of stars, planets and moon, reminds us of his presence. It is his love that helps us to understand the love we feel from and for each other. It is his care of and for us that reminds us that he was, is, and always will be with us for God is the great I Am.

"Gracious God we recognize your presence in everything that we touch, feel, see or experience. Help us to look beyond our present to your eternal, for we know that you have been, are and always will be our God. In your eternal son's name we pray. Amen"

SALT PANS

"You are the salt of the earth. But if the salt loses its saltiness, how can it be made salty again? It is no longer good for anything, except to be thrown out and trampled by men."

—Matthew 5:13

When Hawai'i was 'discovered' by the sailing fleets of the world, it gained almost instant importance. Not only was Hawai'i a wonderful place for rest and relaxation after a long and arduous sea voyage, but it fulfilled a need for restocking of ships with fresh food supplies. As the winds of the world were better understood by those who depended upon them there was continual improvement in sailing conditions. Still the Pacific Ocean was a vast body of water and to cross it meant much time away from shore and a constant source of food.

The preservation of that food which was kept on board the sailing ship was one of the problems of sailing. With no modern facilities for food storage, the sailing ships of the world were dependant upon salt for preservation. The local Hawaiian folk also needed salt for the preservation of food in their warm climate. The production of salt became important, not just for the needs of the native Hawaiians, but also for sale to the sailors who visited Hawaiian shores.

One of the leading sources of salt was the community of Hanapepe, located on the southwest shore of Kaua'i. The production of salt continues to this day in the ancient method of extraction from salt water by evaporation.

The salt pans of Hanapepe have been in use by continuing generations of families who have lived in the Hanapepe area. The traditional method of salt production continues on the flats to the west of the mouth of the Hanapepe River, in an area that has become Salt Pond State Park.

In the spring, when the rains of winter have stopped, those who are involved in making salt will rebuild their "pans". Using the clay of the area, they form pans six to eight feet wide and eight to fifteen feet long. These pans are flat and have a rim or edge around them. These rims are built of clay and are perhaps six inches high. Only those who have traditional family rights to the salt pan area are allowed to make salt here. Though no written record is made of who owns the rights, the families involved strictly observe them.

Wells have been dug throughout the area which bring in the salt water from the ocean. Water is drawn from the wells and spread over the pan. Evaporation takes place until the water is nearly gone, and then more water is added. As more evaporation takes place, the water becomes supersaturated with salt. When a crust forms on the surface, it is pulled carefully to one side and more water is added. Daily water is added and evaporates, leaving a continuing crust of salt which is then removed.

The rims or edges of the pan need continual repair and the pan needs continual and constant refilling. The result is not just a salt of sodium chloride, but also a salt that contains many other minerals found in salt water. The secret of 'making salt' is the constant exposing of salt water to the sun and the evaporation that results. The process involves much time and much care.

The salt that is produced is especially prized for use in Hawaiian cooking. No other salt or potion offers the unique flavor that seems to bring an *aloha* of taste to Hawaiian foods.

God's word speaks much about salt, as in Biblical times there was no other form of preservation except for drying. Even in the process of drying, salt was often the means for preservation. In Biblical times broken pieces of pottery were immersed in the salty Dead Sea and then taken to Jerusalem. When the shards were relieved of their salt content, after immersion in water, the shards were then of no further value. Salt was seen in Christ's teachings as many things including purity, antiseptic, an indication of friendship, fidelity, hospitality and the spiritual health and vigor necessary as Christian virtues in a corrupt world.

It is possible for us to find the true salt by exposing ourselves continually to God's will. With the edges of our "pan" continually rebuilt we present ourselves to God, in prayer, and in our thinking, which often becomes an unspoken prayer. This means God views every area of our lives, every nook, cranny, closet, attic and basement. We must recognize ourselves as a unique being owned by him, willing to listen to him and willing and ready to do his will.

A constant, conscious, exposure to God will result in the purity of mind and heart that God so desires. It is often a slow process but we should be willing to let God control all areas of our lives.

The result is a purifying, a preserving, and an extending of hospitality between God and ourselves because we were willing to make Christian salt in the Hawaiian fashion.

"Gracious God, we admit that we are only the salt of the earth if we have your will preserved in our lives. In the life and light of your son may we view ourselves that we might be pure for you. In Jesus' name we pray. Amen."

TIME ON MY HANDS

"There is a time for everything, and a season for every activity under heaven: To be born, and to die, to plant and uproot, to kill and heal, to tear down and build, to weep and laugh, to mourn and dance, to scatter stones and gather them, to embrace and refrain from embracing, to search and to give up, to keep and throw away, to tear and to mend, to be silent and to speak, to love and to hate, for war and for peace."

—Ecclesiastes 3:1–8 (Abbreviated)

The service in the Yum Yum Tree Restaurant had been excellent, which of course meant that the hot food was hot, the cold food was cold and the water glass never dropped below half full. Every time the waiter passed our table he scanned each of the plates to make sure that the empty plates were removed and that everything was in order.

The food was excellent and it was quiet enough for conversation but not so quiet that everyone else heard what you had to say. The waiters and waitresses moved speedily and quietly, aware of all the customers, not just those assigned to their tables. As soon as a table was vacated, three or four people appeared and in less time that it takes to describe, the table was cleared, cleaned, (even given a rubdown with a special sanitized towel), and reset.

We had noticed one particular waiter who was a time-space management consultant's dream-come-true. He never entered or left the eating area without accomplishing two or three things at the same time, but he did so with seeming little rush. His actions just seemed to flow as though he was programmed to accomplish everything that needed to be done effortlessly. In spite of all he did he seemed cool. He thoroughly enjoyed being a waiter.

But more amazing, on his wrists he wore seven or eight watches, of the modern glow-color variety, giving the impression more of ornamentation than the utility of telling the time. When we remarked on his many watches, the waiter confessed he also had watches in his pockets, under his vest jacket and pinned on his shirt. He showed us his belt and it was created of watches, again of many different colors. He liked to collect watches and why should he keep them in his room when he liked to display them?

Of course all the watches were running, some ticking, others doing whatever electronic watches do. On his right arm were watches that were wound by the movement of his body, and as he was right handed, they were always completely wound. On his left arm were watches that were totally waterproof. When he swam or dived or surfed, these watches were with him and he boasted that not one of them had ever failed. He admitted that if he passed a watch store he would possibly buy himself a present, another watch. Some had chronometers, others had alarms, most gave the date. He said that he had them programmed so that those that needed new batteries were serviced before the need was great. I jokingly asked what his favorite news magazine was and he answered with a very straight face, "Time, of course."

He had "time on his hands", and the interesting thing was that he actually used the time that he had extremely well, so well that we were impressed with his abilities throughout our meal. I must confess that I am sorry that we have so little use for watches. There are several that I would like to have: one that has a computer on it so that when I need one (say once a month) it would be available. I would have one with telephone numbers which would be handy when I'm in an airport and want to call someone. Of course there are many other watches of special use, even some that give you the Ground Positioning Service if that is what you need.

I would like a watch with a miniature radio imbedded in it and one with a timer for running, and an exchange-function watch for changing dollars into pounds, yen, franks, marks and the new Euro-currency. Of course I'd also need a watch that would easily tell the time of day and night, and what time it is, right now, in London, Paris, Tokyo, Manila and Timbuktu. Oh, the list goes on and on.

But really more important is the use that I make of the time that God has given me, particularly from now to the time that I die. Somewhere in God's Book of Life it is determined that I have just so many more hours and minutes left before I leave this life for a better–timeless–life. How can I use that time to the best possible benefit, not only for me but particularly for God? Is it better to rush about doing all sorts of odds and ends, or is it better to stick with one particular project and see it through to total completion?

Despite the many watches that the waiter carried with him, it was his use of time that was impressive. How could I be just as efficient as he was during the time that he waited on us? Perhaps I need to meditate for a longer period of time on the passage from Ecclesiastes. The phrase sticks with me, "A time for everything." How do I determine just what are the proper things for me to do?

Christ's example, at the beginning of his ministry, was to take off for the wilderness and there take more time for prayer and communion with God—and possibly there we have the key. But where, easily accessible, is there a wilderness to which I can repair, to repair my walk with God? A jiffy prayer in the morning and a jiffy prayer at night are not solutions, nor good substitutes, and you can pray whether swimming laps, welded to a wheelchair by disease or weakness, or driving. (Yes, you can pray with your eyes open and on the road.)

Time spent in quality actions only comes when we spend time with God in meditation and prayer. Quality actions come only as the result of quality time spent with God.

"Gracious God, may my union with you, through communion with you in prayer, lead me in the way that you would have me to go, to efficiently and effectively use the rest of my time for the good of your eternity. In Christ's name I pray. Amen"

DEAD END

"Jesus answered, 'I am the way and the truth and the life. No one comes to the Father except through me. If you really knew me, you would know my Father as well. From now on, you do know him and have seen him.'"

—John 14:6

There facing me was a huge hand that had written all over it, "Halt". The sign was a Dead End. I had been wondering and wandering through the housing development trying to find my way to a particular home. Each time I thought I might finally get somewhere, there appeared that deadly yellow sign, "Dead End."

Of course the car had a reverse, so it was merely of matter of backing around and heading out on another street. The real difficulty was coming to the Dead End of a one way street. However I backed out and again looked for the street and the appropriate number that would get me to my destination. I had this problem many times. They gave me directions that seemed specific but always seemed to miss something. They would say, "Oh, you can't possibly miss the house. It is green with white trim," but it would end up tan with brown trim. And of course I ended up with a Dead End.

In my college days I drove from the middle of Kansas to Pittsburgh, PA with three others in my roommate's car. It was black, it was a Dodge, it was old and it had a fine motor, but the transmission would not go into either low gear or reverse. We learned quickly never to get into a situation where we needed the low gear and also never to get into a situation where we would have to back up. That eliminated a lot of parking spaces and when someone parked in front of us. three of us had to push to move the car back My roommate owned the car, we were invited riders, he drove and we pushed. A Dead End is embarrassing to say the least.

Dead End streets are wonderful places for children to play, without worry of traffic. Some of the world's best baseball players and also soccer player got their start on Dead End streets in their hometowns. Dead End streets are wonderful places to park and talk late into the night. But the parking and talking often lead to eating and drinking and the resulting spread of pollution.

Often the Dead End means that the developer ran out of money, or was too busy or just ran out of room and with no place to go, he stopped, put up a "Dead End" sign and moved somewhere else.

A dead end also provides a place of consternation, confusion and conclusion. Writers, having reached a dead end, are finished. They have had great plots but the plots are not long enough to stretch into a full novel, or they have lost the art of clothing a stick figure with enough nouns and adjectives to make him or her into a plausible character. The action seems just like all the other action that they have written, and unless you are writing love novels, where pretty much everything is the same except for the names and places, there seems no place to go. Read several novels by a particular author and you can outguess the author before the end of the book. The author has hit a Dead End and is stymied by the lack of inspiration. The reader can tell that the end, the Dead End, is near.

Hawaiian Dead Ends often end up with great vistas or possibly the beginning of a new experience. The Dead End can reveal the *Pali* or cliffs and what has been a fun drive can really lead to a breathtaking moment of grandeur or beauty. The Kokee Road on the Island of Kaua'i leads to the outlook of the Kalalau Valley, a breathtaking view of cliffs, verdant valleys, red dirt razorback mountains and the azure blue of the Pacific Ocean.

Possibly the Dead End can lead to a beach that offers a vista to not only the horizon but also the world beneath the surf. The cane road that extends West from the Kaumauali'i Highway leads to the Dead End of Polihale Beach and occasionally the barking sands, and the roaring surf. But Hawai'i is also a Dead End in that it is the "end" of the country. Once you get to Kaua'i you are as West as you can go. (Well, you might try hiking out the Aleutian Chain in Alaska but it will be a cool trip.)

Hawai'i offers a supposedly easy way of life, with supposed abundance of food, an easy climate, a people that are known for being accommodating, a people who have welcomed millions to their shores over the past two hundred years. All of these things seem to draw folk who have sought and finally found their Dead End. Then they find that there is still no free lunch, even in Hawai'i. One can live for a while on borrowed fruit but it makes for a poor diet, particularly when one finds that the tree belongs to a native Hawaiian. Even in Hawai'i everyone is expected to be a productive member of society.

Many valleys of Hawai'i have housed the Dead End folk for years. During the "Hippy Era" the roads were filled with hitchhikers thumbing their way from one Dead End valley to another. There seemed to be no rhyme or reason to their thinking. The confusion of the Dead End only seemed to compound their situation. Then many of them realized that work was still necessary and the Dead End turned to an avenue of service. Having reached the end of their rope, they tied a knot and hung on and found that abilities learned in their youth were still viable and so they became productive members of society. Many of these have realized that their children should not have to go through the Dead-Ending relationship that they endured.

Many years ago a young man came into his own. He taught that life was not a Dead End but that there was more than just an escape clause. Instead of Dead End, he became the "Truth, the Life and the Way." His followers soon became the followers of "the Way" and that was their first name for what became a large group. The Way that the followers took was not known when first followed, but at least none of them ever arrived at a Dead End. What may have seemed a Dead End was really an entrance to a new and more real life.

Ever since that time, the life and teachings of Jesus Christ have provided a way out of life's Dead Ends. When people felt there was nowhere else to go, the Master of the Way provided a path that always led higher to a new experience.

The Dead End always reminds us that regardless of how one feels, how low one seems to have settled, how lax ones' life, how confused the intersections experienced, that there is and always will be a way out of the situation.

One has to take that route consciously; there is no Dead End in the Christian life. Regardless of whether the person is young and inexperienced or old and well worn out, there still is a new excitement to the following of the Way. Sometimes it is required to acknowledge "I"m sorry," where there might have been a blunder into the wrong place at the wrong time, but the Maker of the Way promises to be with you.

A Dead End? Is that how your feel? Then welcome to the One who twists Dead Ends into avenues of service. Relax and enjoy the trip. There is no limit to what you can do to help others as they wander the highways, byways, streets, alleys and Dead Ends. We are reminded that to be dead is not an end. The Dead End of life abuts the greatest adventure that mankind has ever known, an eternity with the One who created the universe, and every big and small thing within it. And He created you, so possibly he knows more about you than you do yourself.

"Creator God, continue to create in me a new person that even surprises me with all the things that you can do with my life. Make me a servant, as was your son, for I pray in his name. Amen."

THE NECTAR

"Humility and the fear of the Lord bring wealth and honor and life. In the paths of the wicked lie thorns and snares, but he who guards his soul stays far from them. Train a child in the way he should go, and when he is old he will not turn from it."

—Proverbs 22:4–6

Back and forth, back and forth. I realized that I was watching the fly-by of many different bees that visited a hive nearby and then fanned out to the woods and fields on the other side of the valley. The bees seemed to be engaged in endless toil. I was impressed by their ability to gather nectar. In the process the scouts ranged far and wide, to the limit that they knew the worker bees could manage, searching out sources of nectar. They then returned to the hive and through means of a dance, revealed to the workers the distance, the direction and the amount of the nectar available.

The workers then fanned out to the sources, gathering the nectar and returning to the hive, and the process seemed never ending. If the scouts could find no new source, then the workers could find no new food and the activity of the hive was reduced.

On the Island of Kaua'i there is a continual source of nectar. With a twelve month growing season, the question is not whether there will be flowers, but which kinds of flowers will be available. Strangely, the source of the nectar, the flowers, can be recognized when the honey is tasted.

If the hive is located near a sugar cane field, the honey will have the consistency and taste of molasses, and you might even doubt that you are eating honey at all. If the hive is adjacent to a kiawi forest, the honey will bear a distinct flavor, similar to that of clover honey on the mainland. If the hive is located near ohia lehua, then again the taste is significantly different. The source determines the flavor of the honey.

Let us now deal with human beings. After about ten minutes of conversation much can be ascertained about human beings. Not only in their speech, but also in their attitudes and concepts about life in general, people divulge who they are, and often many times things about their backgrounds and upbringing. The Christian influences and experiences, in their lives, even where they worship are detected in their speech and mannerisms.

The language that we use often conveys more about us than the things that we say. How we say it says more than what we say. As the source of honey is always in the nectar of the flowers, so the source of our living and our life is shown in how we live and what we say, the words that we use and in the expressing of those things that are important to us. How we think about God, and his relationship to us and our relationship with him can be seen in the words and the actions of our every day lives.

The kinds of books that we read, or even the fact that we don't read books, the kinds of TV shows that we view, the kind of humor that we enjoy, the kinds of friends that we have, all are revealed in our language, in our ability to express ourselves. Our talking and writing reveal our backgrounds.

The honey reveals it all. The hive master has the chance to move the hives to different locations, and does so at will. It is done at the 'slow time' of the day and is done as quietly as possible so as not to disturb the bees. In the new location the bees continue their work of gathering and life goes on, but the honey is different. In a sense a mind game is played with the bees. They must move far enough that impressions of former sources of nectar are not confused with the new sources of nectar. They need to know the location of the new hive and forget the old so that they do not return to their old ways. In the new location the bees continue their work of gathering and life goes on, but the honey is different. They may not recognize the difference but the one who tastes it does. We also have the chance to change our sources of information.

Through education and intention we can change many things in our lives. As parents we attempt to do this to influence our children for the right: changing their eating habits, their information-gathering habits their entertainment habits and also their choice of friends. Woe are we if we try to change them without changing our own habits, for youth see through us faster than we can see through ourselves. Our intentions must be honest, our decisions based on knowledge, and our goals and aims determined by God, the "hive-keeper" if we really desire the best for our children and ourselves.

The pressures today are no greater than they were in former generations, they just seem so. We find similar situations in the Bible, written 4000 years ago, and can read that scripture as applying to us today and tomorrow.

The Hebrew laws extending from the Ten Commandments were created by God to move his people in a direction that was compatible with God's will for their lives and also to give the people an ability to work together as a tribal nation. The Proverbs were used to guide all ages in a direction of proper morals. They form a basis for compatible moral behavior even today.

We have much to learn, and much can be found in a good "source" of honey, God's Word. Let's give the proper signals to our children and our loved ones that their honey will reveal the true source of all good.

"Gracious Heavenly Father, I have gained much from my earthly father and mother. Help me to remember and reinforce the best that they have offered me. Strengthen my knowledge of your word. For I pray in your son's name. Amen."

THE LAUHALA TREE

"When the day of Pentecost came, they were all together in one place. When they heard this sound, a crowd came together in bewilderment. 'Then how is it that each of us hears them in his own native language? Parthians, Medes and Elamites; residents of Mesopotamia, Judea, Cappadocia, Pontus and Asia, Phyrgia and Pamphylia, Egypt and the parts of Libya near Cyrene; visitors from Rome.'"

—Acts 2:1–10 (selected)

ulana I ho'okahi	Woven together into one
a pakahi na lauhala	The individual strands of lauhala
I hue a ikaika a mau loa	Become strong and long lasting.
a pono pu na pua o keia 'aina.	So, too, the children of this land.

The lauhala tree is a unique species in a land of rather unique trees. At first glance it seems that it is trying to get away from the ground, for the trunk starts about three feet above the ground and the roots seem to extend in all directions from the trunk to the ground, often forming a tepee-like root structure.

Jokingly the tree is referred to as the pineapple tree by tour bus drivers, because the fruit indeed often looks more like the pineapple than does the pineapple itself, which of course grows out of the ground. To the uninitiated tourist this can become a long lasting impression, for on the Island of Kaua'i there are no pineapple fields with which to compare. The sections of the fruit of the tree also are broken apart and used to make rather well defined leis.

But it is the leaf of the tree that is well known. It is the leaf that is referred to in the Hawaiian proverb above, for the leaves are the basic ingredient for weaving hats, mats, and even some wall coverings, particularly in the 'old days and the old ways.'

41

The leaves are run through a series of sharp knives or razor blades to produce strips that are uniform in width. These pieces are then woven into a crossed pattern and can be used in making many different articles. Often they are woven out of green strips which dry in time yet maintain their shape. Individually the strips are not strong, but woven into a cross-stitched pattern, the article becomes strong and durable for years, even with constant use.

The pattern of the proverb is that when the people of Hawai'i are woven together the final result is strong. The diversity of the people of Hawai'i becomes a strength that is hard for others to realize. Hawai'i is not just one mass of humanity but rather a combination of many different cultures, living mostly in harmony with each other. Our lives are intertwined inextricably with each other.

The only cultures not well defined are the haole, or white, cultures, for they are often a blend of English, French, German, Danish, Norwegian, Irish and others. There are other differentiations within culture groups such as the Issei, Niesei and Sonesai of the Japanese culture. Those who have emigrated from the Philippines have come in two separate groups, the first group being farming folk from the country and the recent emigres being from the cities and therefore possibly more cosmopolitan.

Other divisions can be along economic lines, and of course the divisions can go on and on. But "Woven together into one, the individual strands of lauhala become strong and long lasting. So, too, the children of this land."

Religiously, or spiritually, we also face a lauhala relationship. Not only are there different Protestant and Catholic denominations throughout the Islands, but also many Buddhist sects. The Hindu faith is also well represented. Again, we live in a woven relationship, crossing denominational lines often for weddings, funerals, blessings and other special occasions.

Though God has created each of us different, and we are involved in different cultures, different faiths and different economic groups, we have one God. As Christians we recognize a Sovereign God, but we must acknowledge that other faiths are related to the same God, named what you will. Living in Hawai'i, we need the courage of our convictions but also the allowable love of God to accept those who may see things another way. May God grant us all wisdom as we try to live as his children on the Planet Earth, as well as in Hawai'i.

"Gracious Heavenly Father, we are your children, created in your image, with individual minds which often reach different conclusions. Help us to show to the world that many different cultures can live in harmony, as children loved by a heavenly Father. In Christ's name we pray. Amen."

DA BUS

"Blessed are the poor in spirit, for theirs is the Kingdom of heaven, those that mourn for they will be comforted, the meek for they will inherit the earth, those who hunger and thirst for righteousness for they will be filled, the merciful for they will be shown mercy, the pure in heart for they will see God, the peacemakers for they will be called sons of God, those persecuted for righteousness for theirs is the kingdom of heaven."

—Matthew 5:3–10 (selected)

Possibly the best bargain in the State of Hawai'i is a ride on DA BUS. The municipal transport system on the Island of Oahu, which really is the City of Honolulu, is Da Bus. The system links the entire island for a nominal fee and the ability to make at least two transfers. For the fee you can go entirely around the island, a trip that may take up to three hours, depending upon traffic.

But a ride on Da Bus is more than just a long ride. Of course Da Bus is used by thousands of people to get from where they are to where they want to go. It enables an individual to travel from the airport to down town Honolulu (providing that you do not have large bags) faster than one can make the similar trip by standing in line to rent a car, going through the check-in procedures, being taken to the car lot, driving down town on the freeway that often is the slow way, finding a place to park and then walking to your final destination. By using Da Bus, you simply catch the next bus (less than a ten minute wait) and get out at the door of your intended destination.

But a ride on Da Bus is more than just a trip to your destination. It is an opportunity to see the people of the Pacific. Da Bus is the way that people of Honolulu travel. If you wish to sit and watch the town, travel the H-1 Freeway. Instead of driving in your rental car to the Cultural Center, go by Da Bus and sit with, and even engage in conversation with, the cultures of the Pacific, to say nothing of the folk from the mainland of the U. S. of A. The citizens of Honolulu are eager to talk about their town, their island, their state and just about anything that you have a question about. You can take a professional tour of the city and hear what the tour guide tells you, or you can get the informaton about the islands and their people from those who live and work in Hawai'i and have only an aloha spirit to give to the visitor.

But there is even more on Da Bus. There is drama, laughter, passion, sorrow, tension—you name it. Who are your fellow seat mates? They may be a couple at the back of Da Bus that do not realize that there is anyone else on Da Bus, or for that matter in the world. They have eyes only for each other. They may be a bunch of kids on their way to school (quietly absorbed in books) or on their way home from school (boisterous, loud, raucous). They may be some elderly citizens who merely flash their passes (check it out, if you are 65 or over and a resident) and have done so for twenty years. The seniors plan on being on a particular bus so that they can meet, talk story and catch up on what has happened since the last time they talked (about ten minutes ago on the phone.) Or, for that matter they may still be talking with someone on their cell phone while they are conversing with you. They may be a family where tension reigns, but there will be no loud words until they get off Da Bus, then the scolding continues.

But there is more on Da Bus. You can ride past the best of the upper crust homes in the town, past the lower crust homes too. You pass through the Samoan section, through the Japanese section, through the Chinese section, through the Hawaiian section through the Filipino section, through the business section and even through the tourist section. You can transfer up into the valleys, past the hospitals where the citizens of tomorrow will make their entry and past the elaborate cemeteries where the citizens of yesteryear rest. Da Bus is Hawai'i.

How wonderful that God gives us an opportunity to live in Hawai'i, with the multitude of people with different cultures, colors, languages, sizes and shapes. You will see some of the thinnest and also some whom you hope due to their size will not be sitting in the seat with you. How wonderful that we are all citizens of God's earth. How wonderful it would be if we could all, without exception, know ourselves to be God's children. May our vision include that possibility!

To many the lure of Hawai'i is the romance of the Islands, the surf pounding on the shore, the blue water, the white beaches, the fields of agricultural products. But, the real wonder of Hawai'i is the love of the *'aina*, the relationships, the talking story during *pau hana* time, the diverse foods taken and eaten for granted, the aloha extended to visitors.

On Da Bus one has the chance to meet all sorts of God's Children. Some are old, some are young, some remain silently in their seats lost in other thoughts while, others call to one another up and down the aisle over many seats. Almost all are accepting of others and therefore are accepted. I invite you to the little world that is Da Bus, to courteous drivers who love their job and their regular riders. Da Bus is certainly not a church, but it also is going somewhere. It connects people, and those who ride it are concerned about each other. May God grant us the ability to carry that spirit into the world.

"Loving Heavenly Father, each of us is headed somewhere, and in time, we are headed to you, in your heavenly realm. Give us the accepting spirit for each other that is found in Da Bus. May your Aloha love be found present in all that we do and all we say to all with whom we come in contact. This we pray in Christ's name. Amen."

WAXBILLS

They sat there looking contemplative, a cute pair. You could just tell that they belonged together. Strangely they looked alike; normally a pair have different looks, different markings.

Their white breasts, red-tinged eyes and grey coats distinguished them as a pair of Red-eared Waxbills, or to be specific Black-rumped Waxbills. Officially, they were *Estrilda troglodytes*.

They really did not belong there at all. According to the bird books, (and of course the book always has the knowledge that we don't, and of course the birds don't have it either), they were classified as, "other escaped cage birds." What that really meant was that many years ago someone brought their parents to Hawai'i in a cage and they escaped and have been living very well, thank you, since that time. Here in Hawai'i the conditions and temperatures are such that such birds survive easily.

And these two were doing very well, perched up there, the nest just slightly visible off to the side. Where their ancestors were protected by a wooden or metal cage these were protected by 100,000 tons of conctrete, the entire H-1 Freeway Overpass. Their niche in life continually vibrated due to the traffic on the overhead roadway. Beneath them was more highway and a constant stream of traffic. And so as I stood and watched them they seemed to contemplate life.

They had built their nest on the windward, makai, side of the highway where it was cooled by the trades. That way the fumes that always drifted up drifted away from their nest. Also they had built their nest in such a place that there was almost no siren noise, for the emergency vehicles screamed by on the other side of the eight-lane highway. Their side of the highway led to no hospital, and from no fire station. Enough people waiting for the bus, below, or riders in passing cars contributed to their delectable diet by littering their leftovers. The birds needed merely to drop down to the side of the road and gather all sorts of goodies

Mainly the waxbills were seed eaters and the seeds were in endless supply. The road crews were lax about cutting the grass and weeds at the sides of the freeway that had gone to seed, as this involved setting up cones and redirecting the always heavy traffic, so it was easiest to let the weeds grow.

The odor of exhaust that they lived with was not similar in the least to the odor of the ohia lehua. The constant blasts of air that flew up each time a large truck or bus passed was not similar to the breeze that would normally sway a tree back and forth in the forests. The rush of vehicles day and night was not at all similar to the quiet sounds of forest animals that they could have been used to, but here they were and they made the best of their situation.

Of course they had the future to think of and there were some troubling circumstances. Soon there would be young birds in the nest and certainly the heavy traffic below would not be a healthy environment for the young birds who, needing to learn to fly, would be kicked out of the nest to tumblingly glide to the ground for their first flight.

The adult birds had no trouble with predators. Though other birds might try to get to the nest, no cat could ever climb a sheer fifteen foot wall of concrete. As they had managed to escape the small cages that kept them or their ancestors confined they exalted in their freedom for they had adapted to their environment and were doing splendidly, and you could even occasionally hear their singing over the freeway noise.

In the Biblical passage we find that Moses and Aaron had some difficult times in the process of being called and following through to the edge of the Promised

Land, but they were always aware of God's presence, in the humdrum life of forty years in the desert as well in the exciting times of removing the Children of Israel from Egypt. They seemed as out of place as the waxbills but were always assured that God was with them and using them to accomplish his will.

There are times in our lives when God puts us in places that we would not necessarily want to be. It may be that our ancestors did not will us, through the genes, those attributes that we wanted. It might be that our education or training were lacking when they should have been excellent, or we did not take advantage of opportunities that we had. Whatever it might be, there still are circumstances that we face that we do not desire.

Then we should remember the waxbill family. We should nevertheless make the best of the situaiton that we are in, until God determines some other situation for us. God's grace is sufficient for us, and he is willing and capable to take care of the future. True, we can work to better our situation, or the situations of our children, but we should enjoy the place where God has placed us. Spread your light and love where you are, putting the future in God's hands. The protection of our God is way more than 100,000 tons worth of eight lane highway.

"Gracious God there are always other places that we would rather be, but we would not want to be there if you are not with us and for us. Help us to appreciate the beauty of the surrounding area, the sufficient facilities and caring people you give us, whereever we live, for we pray in your son's name. Amen."

BUCKLE UP—IT'S THE LAW

"The whole city was aroused, and the people came running from all directions. Seizing Paul, they dragged him from the temple and immediately the gates were shut. While they were trying to kill him, news reached the commander of the Roman troops that the whole city of Jerusalem was in an uproar. He at once took some officers and soldiers and ran down to the crowd. When the rioters saw the commander and his soldiers, they stopped beating Paul."

—Acts 21:30–32

In Hawai'i the law says that you must have your seat belt fastened whenever the car is in motion. It used to be the law applied only to those sitting in the front seat but now, it is the law that you have your seat belt fastened, where ever you might be placed.

In the independent fashion of many Hawaiians, there are those who are slow to become convinced it is the law. With more and more being ticketed, though, the convincing is becoming easier. How strange that people have to be forced to protect themselves. It seems they even resent those cars that have automatic seat belts which fall back when the door is opened and then automatically are secured when the door is closed.

Of course there are those who feel if they are pinned in a car by the seat belt their chances of survival are not too good. They prefer the freedom to think they can wiggle out in the case of an accident. Unfortunately, according to statistics, the difference between life and death is the seat belt that is or is not fastened. Of course there are some who prefer to be naturally right and statistically wrong, rather than statistically right and naturally dead. So be it.

It has been established through hundreds and thousands of tests and accidents, if you are in an accident and are secured to the car with a seat belt, your chances of survival are much better. The car is made to protect you and as long as you are firmly attached you will stay with it, and probably survive the accident. Interesting also is the fact when a car rolls, or its involved in an accident, the

50

human being is thrown out of the car, whether the car is in a sideward accident or a head-on collision. In Hawai'i it is BUCKLE UP—IT'S THE LAW, regardless of whether you are a visitor or a kama'aina.

Why would a writer want to put this safety message on a written page? Because there is also a theological message for us in this motto. When it comes to the church we should "Buckle Up—It's The Love."

Any person who becomes involved in the life of a Christian, Buddhist or you-name-it kind of church, realizes that troubles are inevitable. Whenever two or more individuals become very concerned about something there are bound to be differences of opinion. In the Christian church these opinions can become very real, for truly folk are of one family and these are family squabbles. Others on the outside of the Church feel these "squabbles" a weakness of the church and fail to realize that the church allows differences of opinion. The differences are really a sign of a healthy church. It is a sad state of religious affairs when everyone in the church agrees, or has to agree lest they be removed from the body or possibly killed for their difference of opinion.

When Paul returned from one of his missionary journeys the question of whether or not Christians should become Jews, before they became Christians, first rose and seemed to be something that would split the church. Some of the controversies we have today seem to be just as volatile.

These squabbles can be over whether the hymns are too new or too old, whether the organist plays the hymns too fast or too slow, whether the sermon is not inspirational or too pointed, how someone makes all the decisions when it is supposed to be a democratic church, the color of the nursery rug, what we are going to do for fund raising—the list goes on and on.

And there are even more serious matters concerning who should or should not become a member of the group, the sexual orientation of the leaders of the congregation, and whether the church is too liberal, too conservative or just too much. Probably the differences have occurred ever since Jesus told a parable and two disciples went off to a corner to discuss the message.

The ultimate "weapon" anyone can use in a church controversy when it seems their side is not winning, is to say the words, "Well, if that is the way things are here in this church, then I'm leaving." REMEMBER, "Buckle Up—It's The Love."

Somewhere in the back of our church-unique-ness we need to remember we are the group of people for whom Christ died. He did it for love's sake. We are the group who are here not only to be redeemed but also to assist in the redemption of others. God will do the redeeming, we just serve when called upon. In other words, we are not only forgiven, but we are here to assist in the forgiveness of others. We may be spending an eternity with these in one form or another, so probably it is wise to learn how to love, to forgive and to honor one another, now, before we are consigned with them for eternity.

We are to come to God as children, and that means accepting some of the finer points of childhood. One such point is the ease with which children forgive and accept one another. When something happens that turns us off, and would drive us away from the church, let's "Buckle Up—It's the Love."

"Gracious loving heavenly Father, we are thankful that you reveal yourself as a loving God first, and also as a truly righteous loving father. Help us to be forgiving, recognizing that when children make mud balls to throw at others, they end up with dirty hands. Keep our hands clean, for we pray in Jesus name. Amen.

BIBLE FROG

"Keep reminding them of these things. Warn them before God against quarreling about words; it is of no value, and only ruins those who listen. Do your best to present yourself to God as one approved, a workman who does not need to be ashamed and who correctly handles the word of truth. Avoid godless chatter, because those who indulge in it will become more and more ungodly"

—II Timothy 2:14–16

Somewhere in the disturbed inner recesses of the boy's mind things he learned as a youth had managed to stay with him. His behavior now was erratic. His mind could not be trusted with normal information as it seemed to roll in one ear, or enter through the eye, and then it was gone. He still could drive but even that was now a problem for him. Back in those inner recesses there were religious symbols and thoughts which just had to be brought out.

So it was the pastors of the West Kauai Churches found as they checked their churches in the evenings there were lights in the closets. Isamu had remembered the passage of scripture stating when you light a candle it brings light to all around and he realized the closets were indeed dark places, so he lit candles in all of those churches—that is in the closets. The realization of the possibility of fire in those closets never crossed his mind. After all, God was in those churches and therefore God would take care of them. Needless to say, the pastors got all heated up about finding lit candles in their closets.

In discussion with Isamu you realized how deeply sincere he was. He was visiting each church, but not during worship times, to determine how he could help the pastors and the people. It never occurred to him to ask those who regularly attended the churches; he could make decisions without them. In each pastor's mind was the question, "When does behavior become so erratic the subject individual needs help, beyond what I can provide?" No one wished to step forward, but we did watch for the little blue car he always drove and if he was in the neighborhood, we made sure our churches were locked.

Time passed and a new phenomena began. One of the pastors found there were new book marks in the Bibles that stayed in the pews of the sanctuary. However, these book marks were made of the dried buffo frogs that just happened to be hit by cars on the highway, squashed flat and then dried in the sun on the hot highway. The boy had collected these and now was supplying them free, for all the Bibles of the local churches. After all, "He was rightly dividing the Word of God" according to the version of scripture that had been read to him so often.

We could accept there was a plethora of Bible Frogs as the coolness of the night brought them out of the cane fields to lie on the warm highways but we also admitted it was difficult for some worshipers to come to church and find that their pew Bible had a frog separating the pages. Since then we have referred to those 'cardboard thin' frogs as Bible Frogs.

Let's not be too hasty in criticizing the fellow whose mind had strayed; let us be aware that to the best of his ability, he was putting what he learned into practice. Do we, or do we not, do as well?

We are told to be the light of the world, but do we often bring darkness rather than light to the dark situations we confront? Is our general attitude one of joy, and are we known for that joy, or are we a dark cloud that manages to hover over every meeting or service we attend? Does the joy of the Lord in our lives show its full measure in our lives, to the top of the cup and running over? How much more beautiful to run over with joy rather than self-centered hate.

How do we rightly divide the Word of God? For four thousand years the Word of God has been with us in one form or another. The Old Testament record was carried by word of mouth for many generations before being put down in written form, first with only consonants, and then finally in written form including vowels, which were really vowel points, dots and dashes placed within the Hebrew consonants.

For thousands of years people under the guise of 'rightly dividing' have used the Bible to do every possible terrible thing to their fellow mankind. By using various portions of scripture they have given credence to all sorts of strange behavior. "Cain killed his brother, Abel", "Go thou and do likewise," and so with scripture, usually using one verse here and another there, it is possible to twist the truth so anything can be condoned.

Rightly dividing means using the correct interpretation at all times. This is shown under the umbrella of the fact that (1) God loves us, (2) He wants us to glorify him and, (3) enjoy him and therefore (4) he shows his love to us through Jesus Christ. There is your Biblical doctrinal knowledge. Many know scripture so well that they forget the purpose of scripture is to know.the author, even God himself. The Holy Spirit is forgotten when it comes to understanding and therefore in the cuteness and cunningness of our own minds, we use God's Word to justify just about anything. Bible Frogs are the least that has been done to God's Word.

For us, we need to know God's Word. Though modern folk find memorization is difficult, it is still one of the best ways to, "lay up God's Word for a dry day." Have you tried memorizing just a short passage? You will find your mind is not as stiff as you think. Just a little exercise and those brain cells begin to collect not only facts about God's will for your life but also directions in his will for your life. Give it a try. It sure beats having to use Bible Frogs to find your place in Scripture.

"Gracious God we admit that we have been lax in reading your word and in learning from what little bit we have read. Give us the ability to retain and retrain our knowledge of your word. As thoughts and concepts tumble down from our childhood, help us to put them in perspective that we might follow your will for our lives. In the name of Jesus Christ, who knew his scriptures well, we pray. Amen."

TAKERU

"Paul, an apostle of Christ Jesus by the will of God, to the saints in Ephesus, the faithful in Christ Jesus: Grace and peace to you from God our Father and the Lord Jesus Christ. Praise be to the God and Father of our Lord Jesus Christ, who has blessed us in the heavenly realms with every spiritual blessing in Christ. For he chose us in him before the creation of the world to be holy and blameless in his sight. In love he predestined us to be adopted as his sons through Jesus Christ in accordance with his pleasure and will."

—Ephesians 1:1–5

Takeru was already up by the time Michan had washed her face and pulled her hair back into the traditional family bun. They had followed this routine since time immemorial and there seemed to be no change in their procedure except for Sundays when the same ritual was followed, but an hour later.

Breakfast was the usual large bowl of rice, a breakfast befitting a samurai. In thirty-five years Takeru had never known Michan to make a bad serving of rice. Only once was there too much water but never had the rice been like the sand, as the *haoles* liked it. Their devotions were not hurried because they had lots of time at the store between customers. Things were not busy in the store these days since the addition of a large shopping center to the island.

At precisely 7:40 A.M. they were in the truck, such as it was. Years of use, not only for the store and business but also in various volunteer activites of the community, had taken their toll. The back bed was just about rusted out, both of the seats had holes in them, and did I mention that the original seats had given way many years before? Mechanically the truck was sound, though it made quite a sound the poor muffler just could not muffle. The engine still performed but reacted sometimes negatively to the clashing of the gears when Takeru could not get his feet to cooperate. Yet the truck was the main feature of the store. To ride with Takeru when he was either taking orders or delivering them was to experience a new community, even though it was an old familiar community. There were so many back alleys and cross-over paths he followed you could actually get lost just driving in the small town you knew very well.

Only Takeru was left of the original store owners in the community. You see, Takeru still made home deliveries. In many of the other stores you were lucky if the store even provided someone to help you carry your purchase to the sidewalk. Michan would mind the store so the occasional teenager who felt that Takeru owed him a free candy bar was able to resist putting one in his pocket. Takeru had no in-store TV to watch for shoplifters so Michan was that look out.

The accounting books consisted of boxes of pads on which were written bills that would never be paid. Everyone knew when Takeru died the books would finally be closed and then the pressure to pay would be over, but possibly they would leave a large Kodein at the time of his funeral. (Kodein is a contribution usually given at the time of a funeral, wedding, graduation or anniversary party to help defray the costs of the event, especially if the host of the party was not wealthy, and really depended upon the Kodein for the expenses) In the mornings he went to his customers, many of whom could not get to the store. He would take their orders and visually see how they were and then deliver in the afternoon.

Many of his customers were *essei*, first generation Japanese to the Islands, and for them he provided a service that was more than a normal store service. If, when taking orders he noticed that they needed some kind of help, he took it upon himself to summon that help, either neighbor, or medical or possibly the Sensei, the pastor. Sometimes plumbers, or carpenters were needed and he made sure they knew it. In the afternoon when making deliveries he would check to make sure the help had arrived. Takeru was very observant. Nothing seemed to escape his attention and the customers knew they could depend upon him. Often the solution to a problem was to take the individual to the necessary appointment, thereby acting as a taxi, though he would have to finish his route of delivery first. And he would always patiently wait for the appointment to be completed and then would deliver the person back home.

The plantation owners had attempted to provide a complete service to the community, from baker to auto mechanic, even running errands for those who found it hard to get around the community, but that service was now history. For years the plantation kept their own store and expected the workers on the plantation to shop there. They were given credits at the plantation store and the credits were taken off their pay checks and if you did not shop there....

But the merchants had held out and the towns people had been good to them, doing as much shopping as possible with the local merchants, and they had formed a community independent of the plantation. Finally the plantation had given in and closed their store.

Takeru was a man of faith, but also of temper. He had a flash-point kind of temper that blasted forth and then was regretted afterward, which caused him much anguish at having to apologize and also in not being able to control those flashing bursts. Yet his faith was deep and possibly his prayers were more than embarrassing. When he spoke to God you were almost ashamed to be listening in, even if it was an audible prayer. He had an intimate relationship with God the Father developed soon after he left the Buddhist faith. All his friends and most of his family were Buddhists so it was not just a casual interest in the white man's religion. He was seriously involved in all parts of the church, was always at the forefront of discussions and occasional arguments, and was always regular and on time in attendance at both worship and also in committee meetings.

The answers to his questions in Bible Study always seemed to be the answers others, less vocal, sought. He brought his business sense to the affairs of the church and often contributed to those in need in the community through the church. His skill and physical ability are still seen in the various projects in which he took part as a volunteer.

Possibly he is the only individual who was given a ticket for going too slow in a speed zone. He had always driven that speed and even though the highways had improved and the speed limits were raised he was still going to go that speed. He felt comfortable going that speed and no ticket was going to change his mind.

But even Takeru realized times were changing. At the end of the day the constant climbing in and out of the truck began showing on his body. Perhaps his time was passing and he would spend the rest of his days on the pier, fishing with the other merchants. The store had been good to him, though. He had put three children through college and one through graduate school. He had been back to Japan three times, he had been able to house two sisters whose husbands died while serving in the Army, and he and Michan owned their own home.

God had been good to him and each morning and evening he thanked the God of Jesus Christ and the church he attended. Part of his continuing joy was serving in the church where he was an acknowledged leader. Though his store might go, his church needed him until the day he died.

Within the changes of time there are some things that are not changeable. God gives us the opportunity to serve him through the church, from the young new members to the 'gray or white haired' elders. The community may change but the love of God, shown through his Son Jesus the Christ, does not change. There is a permanence that goes beyond other facets of life and brings assurance to those who are active in the life of the church. May God grant us that assurance.

"Gracious God we thank you for the saints of the church. True, they may slip into oblivion in the coming ages, as will we, but the church that will be is the church that is, is the church that was. The elders and those who have supported the church, have left an impression. Though the church is not decorated with plaques, it is still adorned with much volunteer service. Bless each of us as we fill their shoes, take their places at committee meetings and assume the financial opportunities through the life of the congregation. In Christ's name we pray. Amen."

HARVESTING

"When Jesus saw the crowd around him, he gave orders to cross to the other side of the lake. Then a teacher of the law came to him and said, 'Teacher, I will follow you wherever you go.' Jesus replied, 'Foxes have holes and birds of the air have nests, but the Son of Man has no place to lay his head.'"

—Matthew 8:18–20

The faint streaks of dawn were barely visible and the noise of the tractors could be heard in the distance as they paraded to the next field to be harvested. The afternoon before they had been busy forming hedgerows around the field that this morning would be harvested. There were murmurs as the men with the oil fueled lighters talked quietly until the word was given. Then the lighters slowly surrounded the peaceful field of cane and each time they touched the pile of cane in the hedgerow a new fire was started. Soon the entire field was aflame with a roar that sucked in the air from the surrounding area. The soot and smoke piled high in the sky. As the flames died out, small piles of smoking cane were left. The flowing cloud of smoke and ash could be seen for miles. It was a signal not only of the harvest taking place, but also to the cattle egrets who realized that breakfast, lunch and supper were in that field so they took flight as a group to eradicate the bugs that would be present. Dawn broke, and soon folk in neighboring communities would see the black "snow" of cane ash falling out of the billowing cloud and indicating that harvest had taken place.

Within minutes the roar of the D-8 tractors approached and the smoldering cane was stacked. Soon the crane would attack the hedge rows of blackened cane from which would come the purest of sugar for human consumption, molasses and also feed for cattle.

For years the system of harvesting of sugar cane has not varied. Always the question is raised, "Why is it necessary to burn the cane?" And always the answer would come back, "The burning is necessary to remove the extra sugar leaves and other trash that would absorb the sugar when the cane is ground or pressed to extract the sugar."

To follow through the procedure the cane is loaded on huge trucks, trucked to the factory where it is washed three or four times and then ground and ground and ground. Each grinding removes a quantity of sugar, and a specific quality of sugar until finally there is only the fibre residue, called bagasse, left which is either returned to the field or dried to be used as fuel for the boilers. The process continues. To harvest the leaves and other field trash is only to cut down the production of the field. To remove the trash is to increase the harvest and is well worth the burning.

What does this process of producing sugar have to do with us? In the society in which we have been raised it seems necessary to have many things. These things might be worthwhile acquisitions, things that we need for our livelihood or to use in our occupations. The things might be many changes of dress that we feel necessary for giving good impressions, or things that were given to us at Christmas time or special occasions, but things that we really do not need and almost never use.

In some cultures to have many things you really do not need is a sign of wealth, even to saving just about anything, parked in the growing weeds. Possibly we should include ourselves in this category. These things might be unnecessary things, some refer to them as adult toys, that are totally unnecessary for our lives.

It is possible to examine one's garage, or one's attic, or possibly the basement, or possibly a hall closet to see what it is that you feel that you need but for which you really have no need at all. What TRASH (Total Residue And Surplus Holdings) do we have in our lives? Are these things really so important that they should take the place of a complete harvest God should expect from his children?

In a neighboring town there is a continuing rummage sale. Items are brought in by those whose closets are full or whose garages no longer have space available for the family car. The items are washed, sometimes ironed, polished and sometimes repaired and then are offered to others who have need of those things at a less than nominal cost. There is more effort in restoration than there is in sales of the items. The standard of living is enhanced because there are those who realize that life does not just consist of storing up things for possible need some day, and there are others who feel the need of those things.

Those who schedule the harvest have been watching the sugar cane field for months. The amount of water the field has gotten, the fertilizer that has been added, all are incorporated in their decision and when the time comes the field is prepared for harvest. Dare we examine those things that we have held dear, to see whether or not it is time to share with others. Ultimately all we have physically or control, is going to be shared with others and hopefully will not lead to strife amongst our children and others who care.

We acknowledge that there are many things that we now consider important to us, in order to live according to the local standard of living. Radios, TV, magazines, accessible shopping all are necessary but really, how important are all of those things?

We have heard of a discussion that tried to evaluate what the individuals had in storage. The question raised then was, "If the house you live in were on fire and you only had the time and energy to take five things with you, what would those five things be?" Another question then was raised, "If you had to take a long march, leaving your home to never return, and had to carry all your valuables with you, what would those five valuables be? Could you carry them with you?"

That question is not hypothetical in this day and age as we have an early warning system that tells us when a disaster, tornado, tsunami or hurricane will hit a specific geographical place. Days before the disaster we are warned that a disaster may be headed our way, and later we are given specific information about where the storm will hit, and what will be the strength of the winds, as well as the speed of the movement of the storm. Particularly here in Hawai'i where we have had several hurricanes we are alert to the weather. But should we not consider the question of important things in our lives before the disaster hits, so that when the time comes we have the decision made?

Continually we read that Christ had no place that he could call his own. Evidently, when he took to the road and left his family in Nazareth, he gave up his place as the head of the house and his right to that residence. This seemed no bother to him for God supplied what he needed when he needed it. Is our faith that strong or should we have some modified form of value placed on things?

Examine this day what you own, though it might take a few days for you to do just that, and determine just how important those things really are. Can we give them up easily? If the answer is "Yes" then we are ready for the harvest. If the answer is "no," as it is for many of us, then each of us needs to re-examine what we own and by whom or by what we are owned.

"Gracious God, we realize that you have blessed us with many things, as well as your tremendous love. Help us to remember that often stewardship is really strew-ardship, as we strew those things we thought we held dear to our selves, to give them to those who have greater need than do we. We are continually thankful to you for all you have given us and we thank you that we can now give many of those things, and also your love, to others. In your son's name we pray. Amen."

JINKICHI

"Saul spent several days with the disciples in Damascus. At once he began to preach in the synagogues that Jesus is the Son of God. All those who heard him were astonished and asked, 'Isn't he the man who raised havoc in Jerusalem among those who call on this name? And hasn't he come here to take them as prisoners to the chief priests?' Yet Saul grew more and more powerful and baffled the Jews living in Damascus by proving that Jesus is the Christ."

—Acts 9:19b-22

Jinkichi had pride in everything that he did. The "Ichi" in his name meant that he was the first born son and he wanted to be first in everything. When he worked in the fields, there was no one who could work as hard and as fast as he. He excelled in everything that he attempted.

His particular skill was in making saki, the rice wine that every Japanese man lived for. One could take a lot of abuse from the white field masters, a lot of insults from other folks, if one had his saki in the evening and Jinkichi was by far the best saki maker on the Island of Kaua'i. He did not know if his ancestors had the skill but Jinkichi had it and his stills were busy every moment that he was not in the fields. There was always a crowd standing around waiting to sample the latest batch.

The community clamored for the results of his work, and there was never a lack of market for his product. But there were times when his production did not make it to the market. The easiest way to escape back to his beloved Japan was to drink his own saki and for a few hours Jinkichi was drinking to remember his youth, back in his homeland.

Jinkichi was drinking more and more, and his unhappiness turned to violence taken out on those who could not hurt him, his own wife and his young son Ichiro. Ichiro's other brothers and sister were not born at this time, so they never really felt the wrath of Jinkichi's anger. In the morning when the mists rising from the Makaweli River matched the mists in his own mind, he would see the

64

marks of beatings on his wife, and the cowering of his firstborn son, but the demon saki had him by the throat and he seemingly could not escape.

It was then that a friend, who had become a Christian–rejecting the Buddhist Faith in the process–suggested that there was a better way of life that he might follow. With great anguish over his actions, Jinkichi, the firstborn son of his generation, rejected the god Buddha and cast his lot with Jesus Christ, and his great Father God.

He knew the saki had to go. The community heard the loud crashing as Jinkichi smashed his still and destroyed the great vats. Never again would he make the saki that had brought so much joy to the men of the community and so much extra cash to him. (The smashing of the stills also brought great joy to the wives that had suffered because of the alcohol-crazed minds of their husbands.) It also brought anger and finally isolation from his friends who had depended so much upon his product. No longer would they speak to him, he was alone on a sea of relationships and each wave was an enemy.

The pressure against the Okada family grew strong as a result of his actions, so the family was moved to Waimea. He started a small business, the J. Okada Store, that sold food and particularly clothes and sewing materials. Still his friends would have nothing to do with him, a condition that existed until almost the day of his death when the supply of former friends of the camp had dwindled. He was still faithful to his great friend Jesus Christ.

With others from the neighboring village of Kekaha he started a Christian fellowship that would develop into the Waimea Christian Church and here he found friends. The hurt of his isolation from his former village friends would never leave him. Only his recognition that what he had done was the best thing would keep him going. His change would affect his family, leaving his oldest son, Ichiro, a man who stood staunchly on his principles. Ichiro would be a village, church and island leader the rest of his life, particularly after military action in Italy that brought him a Purple Heart.

Jinkichi reminds us that conversion is a 180 degree turn around. There are some that claim conversion is a 360 degree turn but careful examination would show that the life of faith that turns 360 degrees ends up going in the same direction, merely giving the Christian faith as an excuse. This is not a life changing event. There must be a complete change of life, of beliefs, of friends when one accepts Jesus Christ as the main friend. It is not a bad thing to change friends if those friends are going to lead you to destruction. As Jinkichi did attest, there is much of the former lifestyle that is lost but there is so much more that is gained when God takes a life into his hands.

"Gracious God, when we find that we are distancing ourselves from you, help us to make the change that will bring us into your presence. Help us make eternal friends, beginning with you. In your son's name we pray. Amen."

THE HOARY ONES

"The proverbs of Solomon son of David, king of Israel: for attaining wisdom and discipline; for understanding words of insight; for acquiring a disciplined and prudent life, doing what is right and just and fair; for giving prudence to the simple, knowledge and discretion to the young—let the wise listen and add to their learning, and let the discerning get guidance—for understanding proverbs and parables, the sayings and riddles of the wise. The fear of the Lord is the beginning of knowledge, and fools despise wisdom and discipline."

—Proverbs 1:1–7

We had planned the hike so that we would return to the rim of the canyon about sunset. The hike would be the reverse of normal mountain hiking, which was climbing up during the morning and early afternoon and returning down to the bottom of the mountain in the evening. We would be hiking down before the heat of the day and we would return in the cool of the afternoon

The Waimea Canyon was beautiful. There was a continually changing view as we plodded down the trail, watching for slippery spots, rolling rocks and an occasional root that would trip us. The changing colors drew our eyes away from the trail but the possibility of stumbling kept our minds on the trail, if not our eyes. The day had been wonderful; fluffy clouds above us occasionally gave us shade. The helicopters stayed on the other side of the canyon, so we enjoyed the descent to the fullest. Hiking is so much superior to seeing things in a glance via helicopter. We did not envy those who were buzzing at the other side of the canyon, but were merely glad they were there and we were here.

It was as we reached the top of the trail on the return that we were dive bombed. Dark forms we could not identify came out of nowhere. At first we thought they were owls early on an evening hunt; then possibly birds late in the evening feeding time. Then we realized we had company on the trail, and that the company belonged to one family. Our friends were from the family <u>Vespertil-</u>

ionidae. In layman's language, they were red or Hoary bats, of the genera Lasiurus.

They startled us at first but we realized though there were many around us, not one of us had been hit or touched, even though it was late dusk. We were busy watching the trail and trying to get to the top before dark and they were busy feeding.

The Hoary bats have a wing spread of possibly thirteen inches and have a fur that is grey or buff in color with white-tipped hairs. They can easily blend with a tree trunk on which they spend the daylight hours, or possibly they will resemble dead leaves and so are hidden in camouflage.

The Hoary bats feed on the wing, catching insects while in flight, or they will pick them from the surface of the leaves or branches. They may capture insects in their mouths but frequently they use their wings as a baseball bat to beat at the insect and then catch the insect in their tail membrane. The food is then taken from the tail usually accompanied by an aerobatic somersault, and they are off after another insect.

Bats determine where they will live, often in a cave on the side of a cliff, and they will remain in this area their entire lives unless there are predators to bother them. Then they move, as a family, to another area where there is safety. Our bats, encountered on the trail, were at home in the cliffs of Waimea Canyon. Succeeding generations would be found at the same site.

Bats fly using animal sonar or echo location. They give off pulses of sound that are not audible to human ears, but are emitted at 10 to 15 milliseconds and at a rate of five single clicks per second. The echos coming back tell the bat where there are obstructions, how large is the obstruction and whether or not the obstruction is moving and in what direction. Their echo location is also used to find feed. They fly more by sonar than by sight and indeed are safer in doing so. God has provided them with a means to safely navigate in almost any kind of situation.

We human beings may not be equipped with animal sonar, But God has given each of us a sense of right and wrong. We can evaluate with our minds what is good and what is not good, what is right and what is wrong. Sometimes vibrations may confuse us and throw us off but for the most part God keeps our conscience sharpened and ready for instant decisions.

The consensus standard of right and wrong in the United States is based on the standards found in the Ten Commandments in the Old Testament and also in the words and actions of Jesus Christ found in the New Testament. We are a Judeo-Christian nation, and though there are many who do not attend church, or synagogue, there is an acceptance of the moral standard, and often the legal statutes, that have their basis in the Judeo-Christian tradition.

People of other nations using other sacred authoritative works usually have their consciences attuned to sacred writings with which they are familiar. We should not be surprised to find they differ radically from our conscience and national morality. As the Hoary bat can depend upon his sonar sensing, so we can depend upon God's Word to lead us in the right way, to note the obstacles that would hurt us and to find clear paths of passage. The reality of tension comes when people of differing backgrounds meet.

How wonderful that God has provided for us as humans. May we respond to that which is our innate sensitivity as we move through the often thicket of life.

"Loving God, guide us in the way that we should go to show your love to those around us. Help us to understand others but at the same time to never sacrifice our learning and leaning on you and your word. In your Son's name we pray. Amen."

TOSS-OUTS

"Why do you look at the speck of sawdust in your brother's eye and pay no attention to the plank in your own eye? How can you say to your brother, 'let me take the speck out of your eye,' when all the time there is a plank in your own eye? You hypocrite, first take the plank out of your own eye, and then you will see clearly to remove the speck from your brother's eye."

—Matthew 7:3–5

There is probably no more beautiful drive than that which extends from Lihue, on the Island of Kaua'i, to the West Side of the island. There are green fields on both sides of the road that form a consistently changing carpet of green. You pass between the interior mountain range with Mt. Waialeale at the center of the island, and the Hoary Head Mountain Range on the ocean side of the road. The drive is a joy to experience and to remember when one returns to the 80 mph freeways on the Mainland.

It was early afternoon, the meeting had been long and I was thoroughly enjoying the drive home when the car in front of me emitted a cloud of smoke and a cigarette butt on the driver's side. The butt bounced a couple of times and rolled into the side grass. My anger, instantly flaring, subsided. There was no way for me to pass so I continued to follow the car. I did take the license number. Why? I have learned when something seems wrong but is something you can do nothing about, it is good to have the license number if, in the future, it is needed.

At Halfway Bridge, which really is halfway to or from who knows where, a green can emerged from the rider's side of the car, which meant that some one had finished their lemon-lime drink. (It is convenient that the soft drink manufacturers have color-coded their drinks so that we can, without thinking, secure the right taste from the right colored can) The wind caught the can, rolled it to the center of the road where I conveniently smashed it. (I don't dodge for cans)

The drive was becoming less peaceful, but at the same time a question was growing in my mind as to what would come forth next. I had not long to wait as a chocolate bar wrapper flew out of the window. The driver was now energized for the rest of the trip home.

I had a couple of chances to pass this very ancient tan colored imitation wood-grained station wagon, but I was in no hurry and I had expended most of my anger over the first couple of toss-outs. I have learned that such folk are not receptive to chastising by one-*haole*-preacher and as I did not recognize the car, I figured that it was better to observe.

By Omao there had been another piece of paper tossed overboard but I could not identify it on the 'fly'. It was soon followed by a plastic bread wrapper. Meanwhile the kids in the back seat were having fun. You could see the joy in their actions as they wrestled about, seemingly unobserved by the driver and his wife who likewise didn't notice two or three plastic toys that joined the plethora of roadside litter.

I must confess I was no longer watching the cane fields, nor the mountains. I was watching oncoming traffic in the remote chance that I might pass the car ahead of me. I was curious how much stuff they had left in the car and where they would turn off. I really hoped that they would not continue on to my town. Certainly we had no one in my town who littered like this!

A purple soda can flew out of the car just west of Kalaheo (it must have been grape) and a few more pieces of paper followed the can on the hill down to the Wahiawa Stream, though perhaps the wind had pulled them out. But alas and alack, I was not to know the destination of the vehicle, for just before the Hana-pepe Lookout a pair of tennis shoes came out of the back window on the driver's side of the car, evidently part of the tussling in the back seat. The driver quickly pulled over to the side of the road. The kids in the back seat had learned their lesson well—they could also throw out things if they wanted. What they had not learned was to judge the quality of what to throw out. I swerved out of the way of the cloud of dust of the abruptly stopping car and was on my way. The rest of the ride home was beautiful but I must confess that I noticed the trash and more than once thought of my highway neighbor and his contribution to it. I could not help but think of the kids in the back seat and their lesson for the day.

I admire those individuals who will take the time to remove a board, a rock or some other obstacle from the highway. Their actions are unnoticed by all who pass a cleared roadside after them. They embody, physically, what Christ was talking about when he said, "Before you worry about the speck in your brother's eye, you should remove the board from you own eye."

Now the scripture does not quite say that but if they'd had automobiles in Christ's day I'm sure that Christ would have had something to say about seeing litter, as the stumbling-block-trash that gets in the way of others. So, what is my litter? What is it that I do that bothers others? What is it that I do that bothers God? May I add to the beauty of life's highway and not cause harm to others by my thoughts, words and actions.

"Gracious God may I never throw trash into the lives of others. Help me to sense the beauty that you have liberally strewn around me and may I contribute to it by not littering. In your son's name I pray. Amen."

KIMO

"Then little children were brought to Jesus for him to place his hands on them and pray for them. But the disciples rebuked those who brought them. Jesus said, 'Let the little children come to me, and do not hinder them, for the kingdom of heaven belongs to such as these.' When he had placed his hands on them, he went on from there."

—Matthew 19:13,14

We had a fun time talking. Have you ever spent time talking with little boys, to find out just what they are thinking, what their hopes are, where lie their deep inner thoughts? Particularly have you ever talked with little boys who live in Paradise, Hawai'i, where the weather is always wonderful, the blue Pacific always less than a couple of miles from where they live, where there is no snow and no real problems with living?

"What do you like best about living in Hawai'i?" "My friend Kimo who lives down the street—we ride bikes together and we find lots of trails where we can ride and sometimes we fall down and Kimo is good about helping me get up and he is good at fixing bikes and he fixes mine and he lets me ride first and then sometimes he rides first and he has lots of cousins and we all play together and we never talk stink about anyone and particularly not to each other and we almost never fight even though his aunties and uncles fight and we sometimes go to the shore and we hunt for glass balls, you know the kind that the Japanese use in their nets to keep them floating and Kimo can always find one or two and he always lets me have the first one though sometimes he will let me go first on the beach and so I find my own as though he knew there was one there waiting for me to find it and then he can always find an auntie who has just baked cookies or who has poi and so we can go there and get some and she doesn't mind as though the cookies were made for us and he always lets me have the biggest cookie, or the one that is the softest because he knows that there are lots more where those came from and sometimes we just sit and talk story and lie on the sand and look for puka shells and one day we found enough to make a bracelet and Kimo he let me have the bracelet and I really felt bad when I lost it but he said not to worry because there are always lots more shells but I felt bad because it was one Kimo gave to me and Kimo is my friend at school because he always introduces me to his friends, most of whom are cousins because he has a big family and it is almost as though his family is my family because they all recognize me and wherever they see me at school, in the store, at football games, they know me by name and it is almost as though I got a family when I got Kimo for a friend and sometimes we play pranks on other people and if we get in trouble then Kimo takes the blame but if it turns out good then Kimo gives me the credit and all the guys think that I am cool which I am really not because I do not know my way around our town like Kimo does because he can go anywhere in our town and he knows someone or can go to someone's house and he feels welcome and we can pick mango or papaya off their trees and they don't care and sometimes people ask him to do favors for them and I get to go with him and that is lots of fun because it is good to be old enough to do favors for people and to make them happy and that is what Kimo does with me, makes me happy, and yet Kimo and his family don't have very much money but they don't need much money because they always get to go to parties and sometimes he invites me along and all his cousins are there and we are always together and the parties are always fun because there is always lots of food there and there is always lots to do and there is lots of music and everyone sings and lots of people do the hula but I don't because they would laugh at me and Kimo doesn't because of his problems, and 'sides I would not hula if Kimo didn't and you get to see all your friends from school and you get to see people who are very important like the school janitor, and the check-out woman at Big Save and Uncle Louie who always sits on the bench at the corner and watches people go by and hugs them and Uncle Kioki who drives one of those big buses and Louise who is a cabin attendant on Hawaiian Airlines and she is lucky because she gets to fly every day and that is what Kimo wants to do is fly planes, but he won't be able to do that because he has a twisted leg and he can't see good out of one eye and he was very sick when he was young but that is all right because Kimo is my friend."

"Father God, help us to see people as your children and all of them as our friends. In Jesus name, Amen."

BLACKBERRIES

"This righteousness from God comes through faith in Jesus Christ to all who believe. There is no difference, for all have sinned and fall short of the glory of God, and are justified freely by his grace through the redemption that came by Christ Jesus."

—Romans 3:22–24

It seemed like such a good idea—the best of two worlds. Here was paradise, the blue Pacific, palm trees, wonderful warm sand and an opportunity to spend time in Kokee, a mountainous area that was about 4000 feet high in the central area of Kaua'i. Surely some of the wonderful things that he had known back on the mainland would grow here along with the tropical plants that enhanced the foliage around his leased cabin in the State Park area.

His mouth watered as he recalled the wonderful blackberries he remembered picking off those vines back home, so with little to say to anyone else he brought a few of the seeds and determined to have the 'best of both worlds.' Little did he realize that his small bit of nostalgia would result in an everlasting condemnation of his actions by those who would spend time in Kokee.

At 4000 feet, on the Island of Kaua'i the blackberries did very well and the birds loved them. They carried the seeds to other places and then the seeds from those plants and bushes to still more places and it went horribly on and on. Now the mountainous area of Kaua'i is covered with blackberry vines that make off-trail hiking through the mountain areas almost impossible, for the vines continually pull at your clothes, and if you have no clothing below your knees, which is often the case in Hawai'i, those vines pull at the skin of your legs. It results in a dermatological war zone. Of all the imports to the State of Hawai'i and the Island of Kaua'i, the blackberry is possibly the worst.

And the infestation is still proceeding. So far the berries are situated in the upper mountainous areas but they are slowly but surely adapting to the lover elevations, taking over any area not intentionally cultivated with something else, and usually they squeeze that something else out of existence. The fragile ecosystem is strained to take on all the new species and still show something of its native existence.

There is a lesson in the blackberry vines, and of course it has to do with sin, sin defined as the "I" in the middle, found in the word, "Sin." To define sin that way allows us to look more at ourselves than at our neighbors, and not dwell on those things our neighbors are doing that seem to bother us. Whatever your or my or our sin might be, it started off with something small that might have been good or good-intentioned. We are all involved with the making of money. That developed into a need for more of the green stuff, whether dipping your hand into someone else's money or possibly innocently entering a raffle, or lottery or gambling casino where the chances of making **real** money seemed to be good.

Perhaps the small beginning was a mere sip of a social drink as you looked above the bubbles at your neighbor. That sip, however, was continued and expanded to a larger amount or possibly a stronger sip and before you knew it, you were a menace on the highway and a horror to live with, a destroyer of family and friends who wished they had never met you.

Perhaps you were stirred by some infidelity exhibited in some television program or in some great novel, and you realized it really stirred you to look at others as a possession and not as children of God. Before you knew it the blackberry-bush of sexual behavior had thrown you way off kilter and you were spinning into a selfish void of sated self-gratification.

Like the blackberry, the problem started small and had no apparent effect, but it began to hurt others, it began to affect you in everything you did and finally you realized you could not go anywhere without being bothered by it. And of course the real problem of the blackberries, or our own personal sins, is there seems to be no solution. No one has yet found a means of destroying the blackberries without destroying the wonderful natural flora and fauna of Kaua'i, that in some cases is indigenous only to the Island of Kaua'i.

There are some who have dedicated themselves to eradicating the island of the pest but they can not even get into the interior of the island and for every bush they uproot and burn another hundred or so are spawned by the birds in their continual quest for food. But there seems to be no apparent way to control the blackberry, for the predator who would remove the seeds, merely spreads them to other parts of the island.

God has provided a means of forgiveness to us, a means of reconciliation between himself and us and also between ourselves and others. Of course there is action to be taken on our part but that is well established. We can respond to God's action.

Our reconciliation is through Jesus Christ, a presenting of the problem and an accepting of the forgiveness and recognition that we are all brothers and sisters, and forgiveness and forget-ness are real and long lasting. The early Hawaiians recognized the need for forgiveness in *Ho'oponopono*, a system involving the individual and also the families of those offended. But we are reminded that the time to control sin is at its inception, genuinely looking at it from God's point of view and seeking the removal of it in early stages. God grant us the ability to see ourselves from his point of view.

"Gracious God, you created us with the ability to choose, and that way we could choose you. Help us in our present state of maturity to recognize the direction our thoughts and actions might take us. Strengthen us to see others as also your creation, and strengthen our relationship with you. In your son's name we pray. Amen."

THE ROCK

"The earth is the Lord's and everything in it, the world and all who live in it; for he founded it upon the seas and established it upon the waters. Who may ascend the hill of the Lord? Who may stand in his holy place? He who has clean hands and a pure heart, who does not lift up his soul to an idol or swear by what is false."

—Psalm 24:1–4.

The phone rang sharply, it was the postmaster. "Reverend, you come down here right away. I have a package for you." The voice was not one of joy informing me I had won some great contest, but there was an urgency in the voice, which indicated I should come **now** and not wait until it was convenient. I checked to make sure it was who I thought it was and again he said, "Come down here right now." I went.

The package was a small one, addressed simply to the Postmaster of the town where I lived. I said to the gentleman, "It is not addressed to me." But his only reply was, "It is yours!" and he hurried to the back of the post office work area.

Moving to a side counter, the one customers use when they just can't wait to get home to open the mail, I read the enclosed letter. "Dear Sir, A few weeks ago I visited your community and while there I picked up a rock from your nearby visitor's area as a souvenir of Hawai'i and your island. It was right next to the Russian Fort St. Elizabeth. Since that time I have had much bad luck, which includes death to a member of my family, three people being sick and one experiencing a loss of a job. Someone mentioned it was bad luck to take stones from Hawai'i, something about Madam Pele who is jealous of the Islands so would you please return this rock to where I took it?"

The postmaster refused to have anything more to do with the box and the rock so I took it to the fort and put it on the wall, not knowing exactly where it belonged. At least it was in the approximate area and that had to be good enough. The matter was closed, and from then on the postmaster would not discuss it with me. The next time a rock was returned the postmaster again called me and again I returned a rock to the wall of the fort.

It is true there is a strong belief Madam Pele, the goddess that created the islands, is very jealous of her work and so does not appreciate people taking part of her creation away from where it belongs. The postmaster felt because I was a minister, I was immune from any bad luck and so I was "safe" to return the rock. I did not confess to him the other cases where rocks had been removed and what had happened to those who did the removing. I was not eager to get into that particular kind of discussion.

There is, throughout Hawai'i, a love of the 'aina, the land. Admittedly there is much land in Hawai'i that people would find it difficult to love, whether the scrub brush, or kiawi and haole koa, on the various islands or the seas of lava that have yet to regenerate life. Still there is a beauty even in the scrub and lava.

One of the difficult facts of 'cultural intrusion' is the losing of the land to those of other cultures and other nationalities. The Hawaiians have been the best and most generous of any people on earth in sharing their small area of possession with those who came to visit. The climate is such many wish to own some small area of some island and, with so little available, the hospitable feelings are changing to anger as more and more land is sold to those from the mainland U.S.A., Japan or many other Eastern and European countries. And of course those who come from other places have the money to pay the high prices for the land. After all, "Enough is enough."

This love of the land is not always shown in the care given the land. Land erosion is seen in many places, whether due to over grazing, or the building of condominiums, or over-proliferation of shopping centers or the natural wash of the rivers as soil is carried to the ocean during times of violent rain or flooding. There is sometimes a doubt of the love of the land when land, after a weekend of camping, seems more like a garbage dump than valuable a beach or exquisite sunrises or sunset view site.

God's word also claims God's love of the land. "The earth is the Lord's and the fullness thereof, the world and those who dwell therein." This word does not result in a fear of the use of the land but a care given to the small portion you happen to own, rent or use. Though the threat of Madam Pele does not extend around the world, the premise is there, if we do not use the land wisely we will lose the land. With the present eruption of Kileaua Volcano and the flow of the lava to the sea Hawai'i is one of the few places still growing in size. It is a violent growth but still is a growth of acreage. Enjoy the land you use, whether Mainland, Hawai'i or wherever—for it is God's.

"Gracious God, all we are physically comes from the land. Help us to be aware it is given by you, who makes us all physical and spiritual. In your Son's name we pray. Amen."

THE AURA

"For God so loved the world that he gave his one and only Son, that whoever believes in him shall not perish but have eternal life."

—John 3:16

It was always the same. They descended from the bus with an aura about them and it was as though they were surrounded with a host of themselves. They patiently waited for the next bus. Their own peers, who no doubt knew them as they attended the same school, left them alone; they defied interruption.

When their own bus, number four, arrived, they formed a single place in the line to board, the boy always held her school pass, though it was supposedly against the rules, but the driver knew. The driver would be glad to have them on board for together they occupied a single seat and they certainly caused no trouble. The raucous kids left them alone, there was never loud talk from them, they were together, the perfect bus passenger; **they were in love**.

They were seemingly with you in the bus but their gaze was always about twenty feet, or seven years away. They would talk quietly, their words drowned by the continually changing gears of the bus as the driver stopped at all the usual stops. The traffic noise also existed, the garble gasp of mixed conversation, but they could hear each other, or rather they sensed what they were saying to each other. There was no eavesdropping on their conversations, nor did you want to invade their sacred communication.

If the bus became crowded they were as one when it came to giving up their seat for an elderly person, their manner indicated a fine home training. There was

82

no place for heavy smooching, though occasionally after a laughing conversation he did steal a kiss, but how can you steal something that is so freely given? Their relationship was too sacred for heavy petting, it was the farthest thing from their minds. Any parent would give a lot for either of them, or for both of them.

And then came the time for parting. He pulled the cord for her stop, walked to the door with her and only then could you tell which were her books and which were his. The parting was fast, simple but only temporary. He resumed his place on the bus for the next three stops and then he, too, left the bus, hardly aware he had ridden three blocks by himself, along with all the rest of us.

No doubt the first thing he did when he finally did get home was to greet his mother and then call the other half of the aura, to tell of his safe arrival and to question her about what had happened since last they were together, some ten minutes before. Day after day this happened, and those who rode regularly with them knew of their deep feeling for each other.

Time is grinding away until they can both graduate from high school and then college and then they will be one. For they live in a perpetual state of young love, that soft, hazy, easily articulated but never defined, human relationship. Their relationship is beyond the physical and almost resembles a spiritual relationship. There are boundaries established for them by their families and they respect those boundaries, for what they are looking forward to is a much deeper relationship that is in the future. They want to do nothing that will hurt the future relationship and they are committed to it and to each other.

I wonder if that is how God looks at us—with a great desire—a desire for a perpetual new, fresh, soft, easily articulated but never defined continual relationship. At this moment in the midpoint of eternity, in this small sliver of time as well as for the entire future that extends past infinity, I wonder if he desires for himself with us, a relationship as desirous as the relationship of that young couple, where the driving desire is to be with each other, to aid and assist each other, to live life to the fullest with each other, to plan for a long and never ending relationship with each other?

I wonder if he wants a communication with me that does not have to start with a salutation and end with an Amen, but rather is just a continual sharing of thoughts, desires, confessions, assurances for each in the conversation is continually directing all thoughts and messages to each other, and for another to interrupt is almost sacrilegious? I wonder if my relationship is like that—**with him**?

I wonder if that is the real relationship he intended, intends and will continually intend to exist by my creation and through all the years I have lived. Not the result of perpetually repeated phrases, divine incantations or religious jargon, but an awareness of, and confidence in and love relationship with the creator of everyone and everything, physical or divine.

"Loving God, you are not just a functional being in interstellar space, but close to me here in this chair. Help me to have a relationship so close to you that it may seem embarrassing to others. I long to be with you, here on earth and wherever you desire in the future. Create in me the longing and then the fulfilment. In your son's name I pray. Amen."

THE TRADES

"Where can I go from your Spirit? Where can I flee from your presence? If I go up to the heavens, you are there; if I make my bed in the depths, you are there. If I rise on the wings of the dawn, if I settle on the far side of the sea, even there your hand will guide me, your right hand will hold me fast. If I say, 'Surely the darkness will hide me and the light become night around me,' even the darkness will not be dark to you; the night will shine like the day, for darkness is as light to you."

—Psalm 139:7–12

A period of calm seemed to have descended upon the islands. Traffic along the highways seemed less noisy. The surf was quieter than usual; on all four sides of all the islands, the surf report was disappointing for the surfers. The palm fronds hung listlessly upon the trees and even the coconuts refused to fall. The birds were quieter, the dogs barked less and even the roosters seemed to slack off in their responsibilities of finding food and letting their dependent families know.

New arrivals at the Honolulu International Airport were thrilled as they deplaned. That first blast of Hawai'i was always a thrill. The heavenly flower scented air, for the most part plumeria with some pikaki thrown in, seemed such a wonderful contrast to the blizzard condition left just a few hours before. The warmth seemed to penetrate the entire being and they longed to get to the beach, to soak in more and more of the sun.

As they made the trek from the arrival gate to the baggage area they were met with protea-burdened folk, recently from the Island of Maui, anthurium-laden folk recently from the Island of Hawai'i, Kaua'i Cookie Box-laden folk recently from the Island of Kaua'i or just beach mat-laden folk from Waikiki. There was a happy listlessness in the 'outbound' stream and an eager anticipation in the inbound group.

But things were different with those who were residents of the islands. They felt a new listlessness. There was more time spent in air-conditioned rooms, more fans in operation, more time spent up in the higher mountainous area. Teachers had more trouble 'driving' the school children to get their work done, the *pau-hana* time of post-work fellowship came earlier and lasted longer, the surfers spent more time on the beach talking and less time riding the listless waves.

Common to all, city and country dweller alike, was the glisten of perspiration. Though well used to the climate of Hawai'i, *malahini* and *kama'aina* alike were suffering from some strange malady that had come upon them so slowly and indirectly no one seemed to realize each had been stricken.

Tempers were a little shorter, police were a little more alert to possible trouble, the welfare office seemed to be besieged with calls, sick calls came to more and more plantations and businesses and no one seemed able to diagnose the trouble—until it all came to an abrupt end.

The change came quietly, but perceptibly, and was felt throughout the Island State. The Trades again began to blow. The temperature did not change, but the cooling flow of air was again in motion and life returned to normal. It was felt throughout the state but there was no grand announcement in the news. Those who were new to the islands could not understand it but they enjoyed the breezes and wondered from where they came.

The trees again began their motion, there was a new alertness in the air, the classrooms settled down, business picked up and indeed the island life seemed to return to normal.

There come times in our lives when we seem to lose interest. We are still living in the same place, doing the same thing but with a listlessness that seems to stifle all new and creative movement. On the surface there seems to be no change but underneath there is no real fervor to give a zest to every day living. We are going through the motions but the motions seem boring and with little meaning. "I just don't know what is the matter with me," is a phrase heard over and over.

At such a time there is a spiritual remedy that can bring new zest to each day, a new direction to life and a new enjoyment of each moment. "Gracious God, send your Holy Spirit into my life to show me your will and empower me to do your will. Amen." Then, again the spiritual trades will flow through your life with new fervor, and new direction. (Sad it is some religious movements deny even the existence of the Holy Spirit, for in so doing religion is reduced to rote phrases and planned activities with little fervor for enhancing life.) To experience Hawai'i **without** the trades can be a blah experience but to experience the Islands **with** the trades is a rich experience.

The same holds true with and without the presence of the Holy Spirit, or should I say the acknowledgment of the Holy Spirit. We as humans do not, and cannot turn off the Spirit if he decides to be active in our lives, but we should ask for his presence.

"So, Gracious God, please send your Holy Spirit into my life, my daily actions and my long term goals. I long to be alive with your holy breath. In your son's name I pray. Amen."

TIME

"But do not forget this one thing, dear friends: With the Lord a day is like a thousand years, and a thousand years are like a day. The Lord is not slow in keeping his promise, as some understand slowness. He is patient with you, not wanting anyone to perish, but every one to come to repentance."

—II Peter 3:8,9

One of the strangest exports from the Island of Kaua'i is time. Now, I am not referring to watches, for they are made in Switzerland, or Japan or Korea or just about anywhere else. We have no time-makers here on Kaua'i. But we do export time.

Located on the western side of the island, adjacent to the Pacific Missile Range Facility is radio station WWVH. This station is related to station WWV (the H in the call letters stands for Hawai'i) in Colorado and its only purpose is to export time. There are no announcers, no music, no diskjockeys, no catchy commercials, no contests, no sing-along tunes, no hot news stories; all you get from WWVH is time, but that you do get and accurately.

Radio Station WWVH is connected to the National Bureau of Standards of the Department of Commerce of the U. S. Government. Its purpose is to send out on four radio frequencies the accurate time and this accuracy is down to the milliseconds. This means nothing to our own sense of time because our brains are not tuned that fine, but regularly, twenty-four hours a day, on 2.5, 5, 10 and 15 megahertz with a power of 10 kilowatts, you can hear the time on WWVH.

Though the signal may sound boring, for many it is very important. Radio stations depend upon an accurate time signal so they can pick up broadcasts from other places, often bounced off of satellites. Radio stations in Seattle use it daily and think of our island as the home of WWVH rather than as a vacation resort. The NASA folk, around the listening world need to know the accuracy of time in milliseconds, as commands to change attitude and positioning of satellites and spacecraft are dependent upon very close time tolerances. Miss a second or two and the satellite is 200 miles off course and may totally miss the interstellar target.

Though most of us on the island do not spend time listening to the signal, they have QSL cards from all over the world, from Germany to Australia. (QSL cards are used to let the transmitter folk know their signal was received at a particular geographical place on the planet.) The time signal is based on three clocks; two that are checked continually to make sure they are synchronized, and if they disagree, then the third is consulted so the accurate time is always maintained. Mind you, a millisecond is a thousandth of a second.

Time is a strange commodity, carved out of the eternity God has established. It is awe inspiring to think the God who created the universe and eternity, both before we were born and after we were born, also allows time to be carved into milliseconds. When you are young it passes slowly but as you age, it picks up speed until just before death it races and you would love to hang on to it. Time is often based on the aging process and to tinker with time often means tinkering with that aging process.

In Peter's second letter it is stated that a day is as a thousand years, and a thousand years as a day, both the compression and expansion of time. Note in the passage the purpose of time is for men and women to come into an honest and loving relationship with God. In essence when looking at time it is the quality of the experience rather than the quantity of the experience that counts. Just what do we do with the time we are given? Are we putting in sixty seconds worth of distance run, or just watching someone else doing something else, somewhere else?

Many only consider time as that period of the day or night when they are awake, but sleeping, or resting or recuperation is also important. This has been recognized in modern business with the suggestion that persons under stress should take naps during the business day. Then the following period of wakefulness produces better and more creative work for the employer.

If you can read this you still have time for quality living. Do not try to prolonging the look of youth, but use the experience time has given you to help others, and ultimately come into a close relationship with God. To many the realization time of old age has been the greatest productive period in their lives, finally finding themselves after formal retirement.

Through the functioning of your mind, body and spirit God has made you far more accurate than WWVH, and your influence can spread faster and farther than its transmitter. You have but to say, "Here am I, use me" and watch what happens. May God bless us in the time we have left, before our continuation into eternity.

"Here am I, loving God, realizing that you are accurate to the ultimate degree. Make my life productive for you as you desire. This I pray in Jesus name. Amen."

A SOLID FOUNDATION

"By the grace God has given me, I laid a foundation as an expert builder, and someone else is building on it. But each one should be careful how he builds. For no one can lay any foundation other than the one already laid, which is Jesus Christ. If any man builds on this foundation using gold, silver, costly stones, wood, hay or straw, his work will be shown for what it is, because the day will bring it to light."

—I Corinthians 3:10–13a

Normally I am an early riser but this morning I was just an early wake-er. There was nowhere I had to rush off to. I had an appointment for breakfast and to go anywhere else first would merely have confused the day. I lay there thinking, hearing, feeling and smelling downtown Waikiki, the breeze coming in the open *lanai* window seemed to intensify not only the smells, but also the sounds of the new day.

On the Alawai Canal three or four early canoe teams were working out, the coxswain calling out the beat, slowly at first but with ever-increasing speed. Occasionally he would shout words of encouragement to an individual paddler. I admired the individuals' grit and determination—they must have gotten up at least an hour earlier to be out on the water at this time of day. I admired them even more for their determined effort to push those heavy canoes through rough ocean water, diving in and out of the canoes during crew changes, later during the races.

There were three or four people on the street in front of my hotel (sorry, just the hotel of which I owned one room for one night). One gentleman had a plastic sack and was collecting the cans that had been thrown out of cars the preceding night. When he came to the dumpster he rolled into it, searched, and came out with a smile and a full bag. It is good to see a person smile!

Standing across the street were three 'women of the night' who were evidently discussing the tricks turned during the night. I could not help but wonder whose daughter, or whose wife, had been reduced to selling herself. There seemed to be no joy in their discussion. Then a white stretch-limo pulled up and all three got in. Their night of working was over.

The rumble that normally settles on Waikiki was just beginning. People waiting for Da Bus, early morning delivery of newspapers to the lock stands, a host of scantily clad joggers headed in all four directions, bikers out for their morning ride. I felt guilty for just standing there watching the passing parade.

Waikiki is not my favorite place. Possibly I had spent not more than seven or eight trips there in a twelve year period, and three of those were because I made a wrong turn, or was it a left turn, and there was no way that I could escape traveling down the center of the district. There just did not seem to be anything to do in the Waikiki area. The stores did not have anything that I wanted, the beaches were already crowded without my body for people to stumble over. Everything was more expensive than anywhere else in town, and it seemed that the sidewalks were crowded with people who were just watching other people.

A fight erupted in the building across the street; two people were definitely unhappy with each other. I realized that I was not the only bothered person when several others slid their windows shut. The fight stopped when the garbage truck forwarded (it couldn't back) to the bin, the hydraulic lift raised the bin sliding all the garbage into the truck, bottles, cans and other trash ricocheting off the side of the bin, the bin was lowered and the compactor went to work. All the sound of course was amplified by the buildings along the alley.

There seemed to be a pounding that I could not identify, then for a moment I thought that I had a headache. It almost made me want to tap my foot to keep the beat and though nothing shook, I had the feeling that everything in the room could hear the steady beat of something: bang...bang...bang...bang...bang.

At last my clearing brain detected the sound of a pile driver that was steadily pounding piles into the foundation floor of Waikiki in preparation for the building of another building. I wondered about this crazy place that we call Waikiki, Honolulu, and indeed the entire state and nation. The need for a firm foundation managed to drown out all the smells, the sound, and indeed the feelings for the entire area. I knew the process. When the piling was as deep as it would go the contractors would cover it with concrete and a new building was on the way.

Where was the foundation for all I had sensed in the last five minutes? What was it all about? The training for a race, the trimming of a body for either good looks, health or preparation for a marathon? What was the background of the three prostitutes, the man collecting cans? What foundation did the couple across the street have for their marriage or their relationship? Do people who just have a relationship fight like that? Why don't they just quit and find someone else? Are there some folk who just have to fight to know they are alive, to whom the only suspicious relationship is one of love, care, concern and the only honest relationship is one of anger, and spite?

The question resurfaced concerning the amount of pollution we have within this country, and along the streets and alleys of the city. Why do we have so much junk it needs to be picked up once and sometimes twice a day? Aren't there many places in the world where these scraps would be saved and used for life sustaining value?

I found that for that morning my mind was not going to wander far from that pile driver. In all of Waikiki, the tourist destination of millions who feel it is real life, the steady pounding seemed to shake the civilized world. Why don't we as humans have pilings driven deep into something solid so we do not act worse than do the animals?

Of course I knew the answer even before I asked the question. My Bible was still open from trying to decide what I would be preaching on next Sunday and the Bible seemed to be not only the best but the only foundation one could have. Why doesn't everyone else think so? The newspapers are full of stories of those who put themselves ahead of everyone and everything else. Many stories in the Bible show such people and also their fate.

Had I missed the boat by not making the Bible practical? Did the people I talked with both formally from the pulpit, and informally in Bible studies, or even more informally as seat mates on the bus or plane, or just passing strangers, did these people have the same idea of what the Bible said?

It was time to shave and go on about my business for the day, but I did talk a bit that morning to the person I saw in the mirror, and wondered why he didn't have more answers and fewer questions about life.

"Well, Lord, I think that I need to not only talk to myself more each day when I shave, but also I need to simplify my own beliefs and feelings. What makes sense to me seems to make nonsense to others and I don't like it that way. Help me to clarify my questions and give time for consideration of them on my daily agenda. I do see you, and your will for my life and for others' lives, as the only solution to the world we are in. I pray this in Jesus name, who also had to face many questions without the benefit of a mirror. Amen."

THE DANCER

*"Then Jesus' mother and brothers arrived. Standing outside, they sent some-
one in to call him. A crowd was sitting around him, and they told him,
'Your mother and brothers are outside looking for you.' 'Who are my mother
and my brothers?' he asked. Then he looked at those seated in a circle around
him and said, 'Here are my mother and my brothers! Whoever does God's
will is my brother and sister and mother.'"*

—Mark 3:31–35

The Lagoon Lobby of the very svelte haole hotel was filled and it was apparent
there were two or three large tour groups. One group, had managed to get all the
front seats. These folks' soft drawl gave them away as being from the southern
part of the Mainland. They had not only occupied all the tables but they had
rearranged themselves so most of them had good vantage points from which to
take video cassette pictures. They knew there was going to be a good show and
they were determined to take it back to their mainland neighbors. The rest had
35 mm cameras or possibly digital machines, most of which had long telescopic
lenses attached.

It was apparent this event would not be forgotten, though also possible they
would not see it except through their rangefinders. Their tour leader had performed well, had guaranteed they would have the best seats, and except for the
fact they had to keep their heads in motion, similar to a ping pong match, they
were all set up. They were so close they really needed a wide angle lens to take it
all in.

The second group, a very hearty group, must have been farmers from the Mid-
west. There was no drawl but something in their manner, their speech, their
weathered skin and the way they acted with each other said they had been very
hard working farmers and now they were enjoying not only the view, the weather
and soon the dances, but also each other. It almost appeared like a Grange Meeting after a good crop. They were jovial, good-natured and probably only had five
cameras among the thirty-five or so in the group.

The third group sat together on the *mauka* (toward the mountain) side of the lobby. They were quiet, intensely taking in everything. Judging from the quantity of their 35MM cameras, they really did not need to be any closer. Their speech, gave them away: guttural with precise words, betrayed either German, Austrian or possibly Dutch origin.

In between these groups were the handful of stragglers who had come to see this 'free' hula presentation. Of course the libations were not free and there was constant movement as the waitresses brought their orders.

When all the drinks had been served several times over, the Hawaiian Hula group set up the stage and with introductions the show was on. The Master of Ceremonies, performed well in introducing each number, giving some background and also filling the time while the dancers changed costumes between the numbers.

One dancer stood out, the smile always on her face, dancing with almost no sense of exhaustion she performed each number through the entire show.

During the male-dominated war dance her intended war-like movements matched the best of the male dancers, her voice blending in with the shouts of the men. Aha, could this be a warning she was not to be tampered with, she had the ability to take care of herself, and also to display this feeling through the medium of dance?

During the ti-leafed hula the soft expression of her voiced words showed the depth of her feeling for expressing the meaning of the dance. It was almost as though she had invited the other dancers to join with her in this melodic expression.

During the Samoan dance, again with a costume change, she portrayed the solidity of the Samoan culture; whether it was the American Samoa or the Western Samoa Islands, the glistening sand, the lush valleys and the simple culture were best expressed by her.

When it came to the tongue-out shout depicting the fierceness of Maori warriors, she was again the greatest to be feared. For the second New Zealand Maori Dance she was draped in typical Maori apparel, displaying the softness so apparent in the Maori; her singing matched the deep harmony typical of the North Island Maori.

Ah, but she was a marvel when it came to the poi balls! She was magnificent with the four balls and then the six balls going in all directions yet managing to keep all in motion so fast you could not have counted them. Through all of this she was calm and seemingly cool.

The cameras were flashing with their red "ready" lights looking like an early Christmas tree. Spectators would come closer, take their flash and then retreat only to be replaced by others, who were in turn replaced by the first, back for a better shot. There were so many flashes the stage lights really were not necessary.

For the Tahitian dances it seemed she was double jointed at the hips. She certainly must have been Tahitian in background. She was really too good, and you found yourself comparing the other dancers in the various presentations to this one girl who performed endlessly and remained as cool as a refreshing breeze.

At the end of the performance, one of the ladies of the front row group followed the dancer to the dressing room door and when she emerged in a blouse and faded jeans, blurted out, "You were magnificent," and the dancer blushed, "but I just had to ask you, what nationality are you?"

The dancer continued to blush and said, "I'm American." "No," responded the viewer, "I mean what is your background? You displayed all of the cultures so well that I just had to ask you where you really come from?"

The dancer paused for a moment and then said quietly, "I'm Chinese, Japanese, Hawaiian, Samoan and Scottish," and added, "Maybe I'm something else, too." The spectator gasped, "Honey, I think you are wonderful!"

Probably nowhere else in the world is there a gathering place quite like Hawai'i, a gathering place which includes the cultures that have come and been so welcomed to the islands.

These cultures are seen in the various foods, in the marriage and burial customs experienced daily by the people of the islands. At festival occasions the local dress often will give way to the cultural dress of the various guests. Religious events and holidays will show different customs an accepted way of life in the Islands.

Though there may be status classifications observed by those who consider themselves in the top social circle, for the most part the folk of the islands work well together. If there is quarreling, or fighting, such as in the school system, it is normally within a cultural group rather than between cultural groups. If there is a social relationship it is normally between the cultural groups rather than just in one particular group.

This cultural integration, but not sublimation, is also shown in the actions of the Christian church. Worship experiences often include several different languages, the potluck dinners are a fantastic array of multi cultural taste-bud tantalizers, and the social mixing is often seen in the resulting genealogy similar to that of the dancer.

Originally only one culture was the bearer of the Good News; now it is carried by all cultures, with the basic faith as the cornerstone of a church of many different building blocks. May we pour as much energy and reality into our expression of the faith as did the dancer.

"Gracious God, we thank you for the wideness of your love that includes everyone who calls you Father. In so doing, we are your children and we need to learn to act as such. May we follow your son, our elder brother, for we pray in his name. Amen."

MORTIMER AND MYRNA

"Do not let your hearts be troubled. Trust in God; trust also in me. In my father's house are many rooms; if it were not so, I would have told you. I am going there to prepare a place for you. And if I go and prepare a place for you, I will come back and take you to be with me that you also may be where I am. You know the way to the place where I am going."

—John 14:1–4

We thought we'd better name them, because mynah birds have a personality uniquely their own. All birds are different but myna birds so often display personalities and dispositions that are similar to human beings so you have to work hard to remember that they are birds. So he was Mortimer and she was Myrna.

They could not remember how long they had been together; it seemed that they had always flown together. Though they had not planned it that way, they were a unique couple. There was no reason to find another mate; they were happy with each other. Neither knew who mother or father was, nor what relatives were among the flock gathered in the banyan tree, and it really didn't matter. You just realized you were a myna bird when you looked like a propeller flying through the air.

But now Mortimer had a look of consternation on his face. Myrna just lay there and did nothing. He pecked at her, the way that she had pecked at him so often, but she wouldn't move. He tried to roll her over with his foot but she just wouldn't move. There was something in his brain that went mulling around and around but it just couldn't compute.

It had been just like any other time they were busy picking up bits of food tossed from cars on the highway. They had seen the approaching car and adjusting to the speed of the approaching vehicle, in their usual manner they had begun their sassy walk off the road. When the car arrived they would be safely in the ditch; they had never made an error before.

But this time Myrna had decided to fly across the road, for the other side held better bits than the one Mortimer had chosen, and that was her mistake. For she did not take into consideration the car approaching from the other direction. Suddenly there had been a thud, Myrna had spun in the air, and now she lay quietly in a huddle of feathers at the side of the road.

Mortimer could not understand death. They had been so close, stealing grain from the chickens, always one hop ahead of the feisty rooster. Mortimer had been excellent in spotting tipped garbage cans. Indeed they had led a spoiled and spoiler life. Mortimer even found the weakest part in those white garbage bags so there was always a feast to be had.

Roosting and resting in the banyan tree at the end of the day with two to three hundred of their friends, their conversations always seemed to lead with stories told of daring on the highway or food snatched from the slow cattle egrets. But now Myrna was quiet and Mortimer stood with a blank stare.

The wind blast of a passing tour bus rolled Mortimer over and over and he dashed back to see if it had brought life to Myrna, but, no. He could not hear the honking horns of approaching cars; the harvesting in the neighboring fields was not registering. His whole being was absorbed in the quietness of his mate, Myrna.

What Mortimer in his bird brain could not understand, we humans with our human brains still cannot understand either. Oh, yes, rationally we know life must come to an end, and of course we all put that off as long as possible, but we still have a difficult time understanding just what death is all about, what 'forever' separation really means. We console each other, we pass through ritual and rite, we mourn and show emotions. Some wrongly try to hide their emotions and therefore store up neuroses that never dissipate. And, as Mortimer was not prepared, so are we not prepared; or are we?

In our Christian worship services and often in study groups, we talk of death and try to understand its real meaning, but it is a meaningless exercise until we are actually faced with death. Then the learning and the experiencing need to come together, for death will be a fact for each of us. Of course there are some who merely scoff at the discussion, with a few passing remarks, but really are afraid to face what is an ultimate fact. We remember Christ on the cross refused anything to dull the physical and spiritual pain he was enduring, as he needed to experience the ultimate extent of human death.

The Christian faith, so many seem to scorn, is not dedicated merely to living the best possible life. There is more to it; the guarantee that there is a life after death. Christ's words, "I go to prepare a place for you," are as sure a guarantee as is the validity of his earthly experience.

The certainly of death makes the reality of life stand out in bold relief. Each loving act, or expression of service, moving to the will of God, has added meaning because of the guarantee of relationship following death. By living daily with Jesus Christ, to the limit of our ability, we can be prepared to enter 'heaven beyond' with him. As we are guaranteed his presence with us now, we can be assured of his presence then. Though our minds cannot comprehend, our hearts can understand and for now, that is enough.

"Loving Heavenly Father, we stare into space and realize you are there. We then look at ourselves, our place in life on earth and realize you are also here. Continue to reveal to us your presence so we might be assured of your presence on into eternity with you. In Christ's name we pray. Amen."

THE ROACH

"Praise the Lord. Blessed is the man who fears the Lord, who finds great delight in his commands. He will have no fear of bad news; his heart is steadfast, trusting in the Lord. His heart is secure, he will have no fear; In the end he will look in triumph on his foes."

—Psalm 112:1, 7, 8

Those of us who are in the ministry are fortunate in that we can sit and stare and call it productive labor. It takes meditation to make sure what you read is relevant, what is relevant is reverent and revealing, and what is reverent will help those who will be listening; to make sure what we say will be understandable to the lay person, as well as other ministers who may be listening. In other words, it takes meditation to ponder a theme, or a passage from the Bible, to let the idea be born, grow and finally matriculate into the world, and it takes time spent in quiet. To do the job of preaching, time spent in quiet is all part of the regular process of sermon preparation and presentation.

As I sat at the desk wondering and wandering in my thinking, a cockroach, of the flying variety was attracted by the light and came flying through the louvered window. Though not a fan of cockroaches, or even hen-roaches for that matter, they do offer an opportunity to study the opposition, so I watched his examination of my desk, noting his dislike of anything Biblical or theological. Finally, with a flying hop he landed on my arm and walked brazenly up to my fist, which was holding a pen.

Noting the hole in my fist, he crawled in and decided to park for a while. Now he was uninvited, there was no parking meter there, and I have been known to go into a frenzy to smash one of his distant cousins in our kitchen, livingroom or wherever. But here he sat in total oblivion of my reputation among other roaches, totally secure.

I wanted to talk to him. "Ha, little roach, I know all about you. Do you realize you can withstand nuclear radiation in better fashion than almost all other animals, birds, insects? If we are all involved in a nuclear blast, you will survive and the rest of us won't. Do you realize when you are about 60 weeks into adulthood, you will get stiff in your joints? This will inhibit climbing and you will also get hardened foot pads, which means you cannot stick to vertical surfaces. Ha, it is a sign of your advancing age. You will soon be senile. There are other things I can discuss with you except I have the feeling you are not listening, but then there are folks of my kind who also refuse education. They would rather be entertained than educated. Something about, 'If I don't know, it won't hurt me.'"

He soon tired and so did I. He was given the option of leaving, which he took, and after examining some tapes, (from which he got as much as I had) he checked the light, decided it was nothing that would suit him and out the window he went.

Now I imagine he is somewhere with his buddies explaining, with great laughter, how he walked into the hand of Ken Smith and got away with it. ("Hey, he even talked to me but I just gave him the cold shoulder.") But possibly he left me with more than he realized. Having now pondered his stunt, I think possibly I would not be so lax in my reputation-building. "Try it again, little friend, and you may have a different ending."

But doesn't my little friend represent each of us as we live our lives in a hostile world? It seems every secure hole we would enter carries the possibilities of annihilation. We feel, or we think we feel, so secure in so many ways and areas and places and groups (that we just know will support us), we forget what real security really is.

Our total security is threatened by the possibility of HIV/AIDS, the persistent ego-trip of sin (which is going our own way instead of God's way), avian flu or all sorts of diseases that affect the aging population. We are bombarded with insurance packages, (but you have to die to get the returns), with sure fire miracle drugs (that would cure more diseases than we could possibly contract in any ten lifetimes). We are bombarded by the supposed security of all kinds of religious experiences (so that you **know** you are really God's person.) We spend so much time and money seeking security we forget just who has the ability to provide it.

Security is not just resting in the hole, or in the church that declares week after week that it has the positive way to eternal security, where the preacher gets all "het up" and shouts into his little microphone. My little friend was curious. He did walk all over God's word, and also a commentary near by. He found nothing of interest in them, and most people don't either. He did not spend much time with them, and most people don't either. He was just on an evening stroll, checking out all the bright spots and my light happened to be one of them.

My little friend did not return. He had his one chance at religion and muffed it. He also had his chance at real security and blew that also. Fortunately God is a lot more gracious than am I. For I 'blow' my relationship with him oftener than I would like to admit. I preach all those things I have such a hard time living up to. Fortunately, God has as much grace as I did that once with the roach. But even God comes to the time when he says, "Enough is enough." May we move closer to him way before that time arrives.

"Good Lord, my fingers and toes are not sufficient to count all the times that I have missed the mark you set for me. Keep me turned in your direction, and give me the strength to do your will, for I pray in your son's name. Amen."

THE SHOOTING STAR

"As a father has compassion on his children, so the Lord has compassion on those who fear him; for he knows how we are formed, he remembers that we are dust. As for man, his days are like grass, he flourishes like a flower of the field; the wind blows over it and it is gone, and its place remembers it no more. But from everlasting to everlasting the Lord's love is with those who fear him, his righteousness with their children's children-with those who keep his covenant and remember to obey his precepts."

—Psalm 103:13–18

An evening walk through the cane fields is an experience that truly settles one's mind and sets one straight with God. On a moonlit night one experiences the beauty of the moon on the clouds or the silhouette of the moon on the power poles along the haul-cane road, or just the shining moon on the cane itself.

When your walk is in the dark of the moon then you experience the specter of the stars as they remain fixed while we on earth continue in rotation around our own sun. Occasionally you see a shooting star, a visual meteor appearing as a temporary streak of light in the night sky. Said differently, a shooting star is a bit of dust which comes into the earth's atmosphere at tremendously high speed and burns out.

There has always been an aura of mystery about shooting stars. Are they bringing creatures from other planets or planetary systems? What will happen when a chunk of asteroid material is so large it lands with huge impact on the face of the earth? Will we then be united into one brotherhood of the earth out of fear of total destruction? Will we be able to get to the opposite side of the earth from point of impact so we are saved? Hasn't this already happened in Arizona? What impact did it have on that state?

There are times of the year when shooting stars are seen frequently and other times when you are fortunate indeed to see one in two or three weeks. But there is another variety of shooting star. The person has an exceptional athletic ability and finally makes it to the top, whether in major league or Olympic competition.

105

He or she hits the world at such a high speed that it takes very little time before the star has burned out and is soon gone and sadly, forgotten.

God reminds us in his word we are dust and to dust we shall return. Some are so famous so soon it goes to their heads and their speck of dust enters the atmosphere and burns out.

The entertainer has a good voice but a better press agent. There is need for a different musical pace and so just at the right moment he enters the entertainment world and the world falls on its knees to honor this bright and rising superstar. Again, the star hits the scene and within months of huge successes, is burned out with sex, drugs, and ego trips. The star has become a shooting star, a bit of dust that hits at exceedingly high speed and is soon burned out.

Meanwhile, there are stars and meteors that have existed in space for hundreds of thousands of years. The stars shine brightly with light we now know is thousands of years old. Their location is so sure mariners can locate themselves on the face of the planet by locating the stars and their places in the heavens.

There was another star who also hit earth, but at a rather low speed, but that speed increased and the world is still rocking. The birth of this individual was heralded by a star which enabled astrologers to find his place of birth. He led a quiet family life until he realized it was time for him to undertake his mission. But this star did not burn out, did not fade, but rather has continued to grow geographically and temporally to immense proportions.

This star also has a positive position upon which individuals can chart their lives. Cutting across all cultures, the star becomes a beacon upon which the morality of mankind can be charted. The value of this star enhances the value of all other human beings, taking the shooting stars and over a period of time controlling them to usefulness. He also enables burned out stars to reappear with a new intensity with abilities channeled into meaningful relationships.

This star still brings light to many darkened lives. He is called the "bright and morning star." He was a bit of dust but a peculiar bit of dust that, though human, came to show us how God is divine. To accept that star is to brighten any dark night and to intensify the brightness of any day. He does not demand much, merely all you have, but again it must be given, by you not taken by him. Of course Jesus Christ is that star and when we accept him by faith we also inherit the star, his duties, his sacrifice and ultimately his eternal life.

Let us not spend time worrying with the telescope examining a distant star but rather with a microscope of love let us examine the star of Jesus Christ, who is within us.

"Gracious Father, decrease in my life the ego tendencies that so naturally come to me. Let me follow the lead of your son, Jesus the Christ, and intensify my witness to the love that you have shown me. In his name I pray. Amen."

THE HUNTER

"Where can I go from your Spirit? Where can I flee from your presence? If I go up to the heavens, you are there; if I make my bed in the depths, you are there. If I rise on the wings of the dawn, if I settle on the far side of the sea, even there your hand will guide me, your right hand will hold me fast."

—Psalm 139:7–10.

It had been a beautiful evening with the sun shining through the large swells with that unreal azure color. Then the sun rapidly descended until there were sunset colors pulsing around the sky and neighboring mountains. The end of another beautiful day at Polihali State Park. There was still a glow in the sky behind us as we headed back along the haul cane road that would lead us to Mana and the highway and home.

The sugar company allowed the public the use of the access road but as it was the furthest end of the plantation they did not feel the need of much upkeep. There was no need for speed signs. Actually if you looked carefully into your rental car contract, you would see you were not supposed to be on the road. Dodging the pot holes and wash-board areas you had to concentrate on the road just to make sure you made the trip back safely.

As I drove along that stretch of road I had the feeling that we were being accompanied. The strangest sense came that someone was along with us, sort of shadowing the car, and he was. Flying just above and to the left of us was a large owl, keeping pace with the car. When I sped up he sped up, and when I slowed down he did the same just barely visible in the headlight reflecting off the rows of sugar cane.

For a few moments he disappeared and then was back again, flying formation with us above and to the left of the car. Again he broke the formation and this time, we saw him dive to the side of the road and with another swoop, fly up and across in front of us. This time it was farewell, for he had a field shrew in his beak. His crossing in front of the lights seemed to say, "Thanks for the light and the supper!" We did not see him again that night.

Many times since then we have experienced a similar relationship with the owls of the island. At dusk, when the light is fading and they have not acclimated their eyes to the darkness, they will follow the car. When they spot a shrew or some other tidbit along side of the road, they swoop down to snitch it and head off into the field with their prey.

And there have been other times, when we had the distinct feeling that the Holy Spirit was along with us, that we were not alone. He could not be seen but his presence was just as real as though he were seen. Following the feeling there was the distinct realization that we had not been alone, that the circumstances were just too amazing to be our own doing, that "chance" just did not happen that way.

So often we try to separate the physical life that we live from the spiritual life that we live. We seek to see physical results for all that we do, forgetting that there are spiritual results. There are physical results; answers, bank accounts, writeups in the paper, notes of congratulation, yet along with them are the spiritual results. God's word speaks of the Lamb's Book of Life, but is God more interested in what happened in the past, or in the total 'now' of a walk with him? If I have the choice between an evening with my children or an evening spent looking through a picture album give me the evening with my children. Is God any different?

God does not spend his time only recording history, storing up for all eternity the multitudinous records of all those who love him, and possibly also those who do not love him and who leave many messy pages in his book of life. God is interested in the **now** of the relationships with his people. It is true that in my computer there are files and files and all I have to do is call up the correct designation and I can find out just about anything I want about all the letters that I have written for the last many years. But God is interested in present-day spiritual e-mail.

You too will feel the very near presence of God's Holy Spirit and when you do, acknowledge him; a short "Thanks, God," for whatever you have just experienced. It is not necessary to send a formal thank you with the correct amount of postage. He hears your prayer without postage. He is not someone to be used, to be a "genie-slave-in-a-bottle" every time you wish something done. But he is the comforter, the "with-strength-ener" who reminds you that you are living more than a physical life, that while you are living this wonderful earthly life you are still in God's presence.

So, when you do acts of kindness that are never noticed; when you pick up that board from the middle of the road and no one sees; when you send the special card and get no thanks in return, when you say those kind words in response to a snub,—be happy—God knows it.

There may be a time when he 'swoops' across in front of you and you really have a living feeling of his presence, or he may just be 'up there along side of you, out of physical view' but he is present with you. It is a promise that Christ made to us, and just as solid as any other promise delivered to his loved ones. Enjoy his presence—he enjoys yours!

"Creator God, I am glad that you are in charge. Many of the challenges that I face seem impossible and yet with you all things are possible. Not only be present with me, but let me feel your presence not that I will glory in it but glory in the fact that you are a loving Father, ever present with us through thick and thin. This I pray in your son's name. Amen."

FLIGHT 243

"Therefore I will give him a portion among the great, and he will divide the spoils with the strong, because he poured out his life unto death, and was numbered with the transgressors. For he bore the sin of many, and made intercession for the transgressors."

—Isaiah 53:12

The Hilo gate attendant called for the departure of Aloha Flight 243, as usual. People crowded to be first in line so that they could choose the front of the plane for seats, as usual. The front seats offered a better view, they thought, for seeing the scenery and also for taking pictures as it was a beautiful day. Taking pictures is easier with no wing in the way, though the wing is still necessary to get the plane off the runway. The tickets were taken and the flight was boarded by a normal group of Hawaiians along with a sprinkling of tourists, as usual.

The folks were greeted at the cabin door of the plane by the chief flight attendant, who was recognized by many regular passengers. They selected their seats and immediately stowed their carry-on luggage in the overhead bin or under the seats in front of them, took their seats and fastened their seat belts, as usual.

The cabin door closed and the safety announcement was made by the flight attendants but few people really actually watched the attendants as they demonstrated the safety equipment aboard the flight, as usual. Many of the passengers could probably repeat the announcement by heart, they had flown so many times between the islands and on other flights.

The pilot checked the instrument panel for take-off procedure; the co-pilot also checked the instruments, as usual. The pilots and the flight attendants were a highly experienced crew.

The tower gave permission to move to the runway, and then permission to take off, as usual. A final glance at the instruments and the take-off roll catapulted the flight to about 185 miles per hour and the pilot pulled back on the wheel and lifted the plane gracefully into the sky, as usual. They headed toward Honolulu and climbed to the assigned flight altitude of 23, 000 feet, as usual. The chief flight attendant moved into the galley to begin serving the passengers, as usual. And then the usual was suddenly exploded into the unusual.

Flight 243 lost the forward part of its cabin roof at 23,000 feet, highly unusual. With the violent decompression the chief flight attendant, who was a highly unusual person, a long time employee with a sparkling personality, who loved her job and the folk that she served, was pulled by the air pressure out of the cabin.

The pilot and the co-pilot could not tell exactly what had happened and they could not leave their seats to find out. They did know that the flight attitude of the plane had changed violently and the pilot struggled to maintain a flight status. The co-pilot calmly radioed their plight and asked permission to land at Maui, her voice sure and steady, and the pilot began the descent.

Meanwhile in the main cabin luggage that had been in the overhead bins in the forward part of the compartment along with everything under all the seats, blew around the cabin at super-hurricane speed, removing everything not strapped down. Everything that had been resting on the seats, glasses, purses and magazines, became part of the mass tornado. Fortunately all the passengers had kept their seat belts fastened. Terminal thoughts and prayers passed the minds and lips of most of those present. The thought kept passing through their minds, "No plane could land with this kind of damage!" But the Boeing 737 descended at the will of the pilot and co-pilot who did not want to change speed settings too much as long as they had control. With seeming ease the plane approached the field and settled onto the runway and came to rest on the end of the runway as emergency vehicles trailed along.

Immediately the flight crew helped the passengers to waiting aid trucks and the modern day miracle was almost over. One beloved flight attendant had been lost, but the rest of the passengers and crew were safe. Possibly hundreds of thousands of future travelers were safer because the condition of heavily used and possibly fatigued aircraft was immediately made very real. An added miracle was that there had been no babes in arms on the flight as nearly everything not strapped down whirled around the cabin and out with the blast of air.

Hawaiian aircraft have the most cycles of flight of possibly any aircraft in the world. A cycle is a take-off and landing and because the flight times between the islands are so short, they have more cycles per day than other aircraft in the world. A rigorous examination followed of all aircraft used in Hawai'i.

There are times when things go along as usual in the life of the church. We take not even a second thought. But then comes a time when something happens that threatens our faith, when the denomination takes a stand that is highly unpopular, when some scandal casts a shadow of doubt over the church, when there is a theological eruption that would scold a few and scald the many. Such is the time when we need to keep our "seat belts of faith fastened."

The easiest thing to do is to abandon the church, to righteously go somewhere else and add our condemnation to the official condemnation of the church. The hardest thing to do is to stay seated in the sacred throng, forgive those who are repentant and live with fervor the life of reconciliation.

A former Boeing engineer once made the remark that he, "would never fly in a plane that was not a Boeing because they are built tough." The church of Jesus Christ is tougher. It has withstood thousands of years of controversy, misunderstanding, persecution and claims of prejudice. After all, the Christ who is the head of the church suffered persecution and ultimately death on a cross, and it was not the 'end' of the church, but rather it was the beginning, the commencement.

God grant us the ability to stay with Christ who did not and does not abandon the church. Christ is our judge, Christ is our savior, let Christ make the decision, stay with Christ.

"Gracious God, help us, your children. As long as there are two or more of us we are going to disagree on something, and the basis of our disagreements will be your Word, which each side will claim as authoritative. Help us to trust not only your Son but also your will as we stay seated in our place, to continue to actively serve you, even in our differences. Bless those who lead our churches of today. In your son's name we pray. Amen."

TENTING TONIGHT

"But they, our forefathers, became arrogant and stiff-necked, and did not obey your commands. They refused to listen and failed to remember the miracles you performed among them. They became stiff-necked and in their rebellion appointed a leader in order to return to their slavery. But you are a forgiving God, gracious and compassionate, slow to anger and abounding in love. Therefore you did not desert them, even when they cast for themselves an image of a calf and said, 'This is your god, who brought you up out of Egypt' or when they committed awful blasphemies."

—Nehemiah 9:16–18

With the expanding of the frontier as colonists moved westward across the United States there was an isolation that seemed inevitable as farm families settled land, removed trees and prepared for crops, first for individual survival and ultimately for cash sale to others.

Because many of the colonists had come to America for religious reasons there was a desire to have some form of established religion to serve the early pioneers. So it was that an occasional evangelist or other person of organized religious training would come into a community, albeit scattered, and put up announcements, usually nailed to obvious trees announcing that there would be a "Tenting Tonight" meeting at some centralized location. He would then unpack a large tent, cut logs to be used as the bases of plank seating, possibly cut the grass in the tent area, or provide straw to be used as a carpet, set up a pump organ and prepare for all who would come.

The hymns were the old favorites that the colonists had left behind years ago, and the preaching was usually highly evangelistic. The purpose of the meeting was to present a Christian emphasis to a life that had been given over to hard physical farm labor.

The meetings almost always began with a potluck dinner, with everyone producing the most delectable dish that the family knew. It was a time of high fellowship, a time when laughter was the order of the day. The children present, whose playmates for months had been restricted to members of the isolated families, had an opportunity to learn how to play with others.

Older youth had a chance to view other young people either for athletic contests or even just to realize that some neighboring girl or boy was very attractive. When dark came the coal oil lamps would be lit and the evangelist would attempt to bring his flock into a new awareness of the Christian faith and its opportunities and obligations. If rain threatened, and often it did in the later evening, then all would move into the evangelist's tent and the meeting would continue. Lightning produced a flash-bulb atmosphere that made the colonists move closer to each other, and that was deliciously fine when you happened to be sitting next to an attractive young woman. When all the activities were over, the families would repair to their own tents and look forward to activities that would continue the next day. These tenting experiences also gave an opportunity for the farmers to discuss their crops and how their labors could be made easier and more productive.

Finally late Sunday afternoon, things would be packed up, farewells would be said and the families would head for their homes and the chores they had left behind. The evangelist would pack up his tent and move off to another place of gathering. If the meetings had been very well attended there would be a possibility that the evangelist might return to the community to set up a regular church, (normally in the tent, that was used only when rain threatened,) and become the spiritual servant of what might become a town of the future.

"Tenting Tonight" therefore was not just a spiritual revival, but also a forming of a community that might in the future become a town or even a city. It was also an opportunity for those of the Indian community, that the farming community was displacing, to be present and mingle in a shared experience. Very occasionally the evangelist would move into an Indian settlement and there share his Gospel. In essence, "Tenting Tonight" brought new life to communities that knew only hard physical farming labor.

Now, let's move into the tropical climate of Hawai'i. With favorable climate and also rainfall, Hawai'i became a place where everything seemed to grow. This also included insects of all sorts and sizes.

When the early missionary settlers moved into the Hawaiian scene, they brought houses of clapboard, those houses done up in bundles of siding, beams, and lumber of all sizes. As there were no unloading facilities for the ships, the bundles were off-loaded into the salt water and towed to shore where they would be broken apart and the lumber then stacked in preparation for construction. This process was not fast, so often the lumber was in the salt water for several days or even a month or so.

This meant that the lumber, when it was hauled ashore, had been impregnated with salt water. The lumber, so treated, became termite-proofed and when the houses were built they consisted of termite-treated wood. Many of the houses so built are still standing without any termite damage. Some of the trees, and therefore lumber, grown in Hawai'i over the years became so hard that it was impervious to termites. Koa, a particularly beautiful wood, is termite-proofed.

As waterfront facilities improved, the new lumber used in Hawai'i, was off-loaded to docks, and not termite proofed, (though termite proofing service was and is available). Therefore we find in our house the following: streams of big ants and small ants that need traffic lights to control their direction, cockroaches and hen-roaches that claim ownership of your house, crickets that take over your hearth and every other place, termites that infest and ingest every possible piece of edible wood, at their discretion. Dare I add to the list the field shrews, other mice and occasional rats that hurry and scurry during the night-time hours.

The solution, then, is that we are "Tenting Tonight." Edible foods and plants are removed from the house. The neighbors are informed so that they can bring anything that they want termite proofed into the house for the gas experience. Skilled workers completely cover the house with tarpaulins that are sealed by weights at ground level and are then sealed at all seams by large clips, until a complete 'tent' is formed. The foreman then checks the house to make sure that every living thing (except the termites) has been removed and the house tent is sealed.

With warning signs posted, poison gas is pumped into the tent and stays there overnight. In essence the gas has provided death to all within the home. Driving through the residential sections of the Islands it is normal to see an occasional house or building that has been termite tented.

We have often wished that we could be 'tented' to remove some of the negative thoughts, words and actions that infest our life. Oh, those infestations do not all come at once, but over a period of time they seem to gather until we realize that something needs to be done. Then we stumble across the word, "forgiveness." In Hawaiian the word is *ho'oponopono*. The concept is inter-cultural.

Nehemiah experienced the need for forgiveness. Speaking of the children of Israel, who had gone off doing their own thing he acknowledged that God was still their God and was a forgiving person. The need for forgiveness was not only personal but also community-wide. There are many areas where we acknowledge the need for forgiveness even today in the cosmopolitan Twenty-first Century.

Along with forgiveness is the concept of forgetfulness, intentionally forgetting something that needs to be forgotten. When forgiveness is complete it should no longer cast a shadow. Weekly worship allows one to experience forgiveness and reminds us that forgiveness is complete, not only because we want it, but also because God wants it.

"Good Lord, tent my life that those things that are negative and which hurt you and our relationship might be removed and provide, then, a new experience of love and concern in my life for you, and your concerns and for your people. In Jesus name I pray. Amen."

KING KAMEHAMEHA SIGNS

"'I tell you the truth, the man who does not enter the sheep pen by the gate, but climbs in by some other way, is a thief and a robber. The man who enters by the gate is the shepherd of his sheep.' Therefore Jesus said again, 'I tell you the truth, I am the gate for the sheep. All who ever came before me were thieves and robbers but the sheep did not listen to them.'"

—John 10:1, 2, 7, 8

Ah, yes, we understand your frustration when you drive on the roads and highways of Kaua'i for the first time. Of course you must realize that the locals have many different driving habits that can be exasperating, to say the least. There are those who have driven the highways for fifty years at 35 miles per hour, and they are not going to change their speed, either upwards on the highways or downwards through the towns. The 35 mph is the speed they will maintain. We ask your patience with them; they are our elders, we respect their habits.

Then there are those who came from the 'Old Country' where the streets were very narrow. When you wanted to make a turn, you had to swing over into the opposite lane in order to navigate the corner. Of course the person behind you, or the one coming toward you, might not understand what you are doing. (When they drove in the 'Old Country' there were no directional signals on the cars, so why use them now?)

And then you must be aware of our 'rock-bound' teenagers who, because they are used to island driving, will go around and around some particular object, a school, a liquor store, a local hangout or just a beautiful girl. Once they are on a highway they have to stretch that gas-pedal-foot so there is an acceleration of speed. They like to appear Hawaiian, so the usual mode is to stick your hand, arm or any other part of their body which may be handy, out the window. This makes for very 'cool' feelings and with it being so warm in Hawai'i, it is good to be cool at times.

Of course we must be aware of the plantation vehicles that use the highway. The drivers are always very courteous and will pull over every chance they get to allow the traffic to get by. Please note that they have a big load and need to keep up to speed, so if one is behind you and you are viewing the scenery, please pull over and allow them by. They have seen the scenery often and they do have a schedule to keep. You may be on vacation, but they are working and time means money.

They will drive as much as possible on the haul-cane roads to free the highway to other traffic. The haul-cane roads are very private and haul-cane trucks move fast on such roads so for the sake of your life, please stay off those roads! For the most part the haul-cane roads are one way. If you get on one going the wrong way there is trouble, and you are that trouble. It is almost impossible for the loaded trucks to stop on a dime, to say nothing of a nickel.

We recognize that there is so much beauty to behold on the island, whether you look *mauka* (to the mountains) or *makai* (toward the ocean) you will probably slow down or even pull off to get just that right photo. That's fine; we hope you enjoy yourself! Possibly you will explore some of the smaller towns where we have *keiki*, children, who think that their street is their playground. We love our children and know that if you meet any of them that you will too.

Because there is so much to see, the visitor's bureau has given the new-to-Kaua'i drivers a help, a King Kamehameha sign which designates something of special interest to visitors. Of course many of these are not necessary as the beauty is so obvious, but there are other hidden island features and we want to make sure that your attention is drawn to those also. So the signs really serve a double purpose, first of calling your attention to something special and also then of reminding the driver that the land first belonged to Hawaiians and most of the land to King Kamehameha.

Occasionally someone will duplicate one of those signs, and use it for a house sign. Seldom are the official signs removed from their intended place. Community signs may be stolen, other signs may be damaged, but the King Kamehameha signs seem to weather all the hurricanes of human possession and stand as a constant reminder that here is something important to behold.

In the New Testament Jesus Christ found the need for signs such as the King Kamehameha signs. They are often found in the Greek and also the English translations. In various translations they are "verily, verily" or "behold, behold" or "Lord, Lord" and indicate that something very important is about to be said or will take place. In more modern versions of the Bible they translate through as "I say unto you" or "I tell you the truth." Then our ears should perk up, our minds come out of involuntary retirement, our bodies sit on the edge of our seats and we should pay attention.

In our lives God also gives us King Kamehameha signs that call to our attention that something important is about to happen, and we'd better wake up to the fact. It may be a medical exam that is not as good as we expected. It might be a pain that we never felt before but which serves as a warning. It might be a community problem that comes to our attention, with seemingly no one to do anything about. But the sign is important and it calls for action. God is giving us a warning that something is going to happen, or should happen, if we are to continue on in the same direction, and it is to our advantage to take note of the sign and do something. Thank God for the Kamehameha signs in our spiritual lives found in his word and for the signs in our lives that extend our service for him on this planet.

"Frankly, Father God, we thank you for those signs that you put in front of us, which we occasionally ignore, and to which we should pay attention. Each morning when we wake and each evening when we retire to our beds, we need to check those signs and then check in with you in prayer. Thanks for the bodies and the lives that you have given us. May we use them to your best advantage. In your son's name we pray. Amen."

THE WIND-SPIRIT CHIMES

"In the beginning God created the heavens and the earth. Now the earth was formless and empty, darkness was over the surface of the deep, and the Spirit of God was hovering over the waters."

—Genesis 1:1,2

On the far horizon the clouds scudded across the sky. The wind-spirit was apparent even at that fifty mile distance. Oh, one had to sit and watch, to ponder and sometimes almost imagine but from the east to the west the movement was apparent.

Several miles distant the wind-spirit could be seen ruffling the water on the ocean, like fields of wheat. Each inch of surface was affected and from a distance, the furrows of wind-spirit could be traced along the surface, even to the place where the calmness of the ocean was pushed by the shallowing sand bottom to form waves.

On the hill the wind-spirit could be seen in the bending of branch and palm frond as tentacles of air twisted through the grove of trees. With patience one could see the paths, follow the highway of the wind-spirits as they wound up through palisades and then wended their way through the trees.

On the pool just next to the house, the forces of the wind-spirit could be traced on the water's surface. Fingers of force created miniature waves that danced across the pool, destroyed the reflection of the neighborhood on their way and created an imitation of the mighty waves surging across the vast Pacific.

On the *lanai* the wind sock changed from slight movement to a bell-like tingling stretch as the wind-spirit danced through the area. From silent and slight movement to a stretched-out stocking-indicator the sock revealed each breath in a never-ending dance that changed with each gust.

By the window the wind-spirit played on the wind-spirit chime. Five innocent tubes hung by five threads, each chime a different length. The striker affected by a flat piece of wood would move, seemingly indiscriminately, among the five chimes creating a tune that no symphony writer could capture, and to which no poet could match words for song. The tune, always differing, betrayed a creator who laughed at creating everything and everyone different so that when the wind-spirit moved a different tune-tone was produced.

On the far historical, and even seemingly hysterical, horizon of God's word the spirit-wind was apparent. To the Hebrew it was called *Ruah*, and of course it was deep and guttural. But the spirit-wind could be seen in Abraham, and his trust in God, and the fathers of the faith, Isaac, Jacob, Joseph, Moses, on down through those early centuries. Having little but a few stories handed down through the years, on which to base their faith, they would match their faith with each other and the spirit-wind would guide them. It was the same wind, air in action, and they could gauge their receptivity to the wind as they sensed their receptivity to the spirit of God.

In the New Testament times the Spirit-wind came upon Jesus, the son of Joseph and Mary. He spoke much about the *pneuma,* that mysterious person of the Trinity that would be a comforter (with strength) for each person of the faith. There were many who were not of the faith but knew that God had affected them some way, somehow, somewhere. They would call that 'affecting' either miracles, or angel intervention or just chance. Of course there was the witness of the Old Testament, the only scripture they had at the time, but the Holy Spirit-wind was still charting a new, untried course. Not only was the course new, but the old sacrificial course had to be forgotten, or rather become a foundation for the new moving of the Spirit-wind.

For the early church fathers there was more hope and more frustration as the Spirit-wind seemed to wend this way and that. Just when you knew which direction he was going, the direction seemed to change and each change was valid. He seemed un-chartable and that was the marvel of his unique power.

On into the present century the dancing of the Spirit-wind on the waters of the world shows the sensitive smile of God over his creation. From the certainty of nuclear confusion to the tremendous changes in geographical boundaries, the Spirit-wind has shown God's force at work in the world. Possibly the present is too near us to understand how the Spirit-wind is working, for we who are supposed to be sensitive are caught up in the glow of rightness rather than the glory of God-li-ness at work in the world.

And so we hear the tingling of God's Spirit-wind at work in the world. Enemies are eager for God's word to them to possibly bring them together. The falsity of egocentric faith is displayed throughout the world. We are given the opportunity to work with God's Spirit-wind, to be sensitive to needs, alert to soft cries, challenged by selfish concepts, and the Spirit-wind is with us; or are we with him?

And now I sit in the refreshing breeze, and allow the Spirit-wind to cool my brow. The mighty wind that has powered God's actions in the world is not available for me to use, but is available to use me. It is through prayer that I place myself into his direct path. Each of us is a slender tube that stands (or hangs) ready to sound at the touch of the Master's beck or call.

And where and when will he call, either for you or for me? That is his decision. My decision is only to be ready, to go where and when and how he wishes. I do know that my single tone will be part of a great chiming. I may not understand the tune but then when did one single note understand the mighty working of the great conductor or composer? My task is to keep my one single note free from rust, corrosion and confusion. I invite you to join me at the great chime!

"Here am I, Gracious God, ready to do your will. Keep my one note ready for instant action and celestial beauty only at the discretion of your Spirit-wind. Give me great joy in blending with others the one tone that I have to your honor and glory, for I am dedicated to you. In your son's name I pray. Amen"

PEACOCK PARADE

"Bless those who persecute you; bless and do not curse. Rejoice with those who rejoice, mourn with those who mourn. Live in harmony with one another. Do not be proud, but be willing to associate with people of low position. Do not be conceited."

—Romans 12:14–16

Join me, won't you, for the Peacock Parade. The parade takes place each weekday morning during the months that school is in session. Few days are exceptions. The parade has a regular route, established through years and years of practice and tradition. If you break the tradition you are automatically disqualified. It involves a short block portion of the Kaumauauli'i Highway, up Ola Street (which means heavenly being) through a two block section of a one-way street that determines the direction of the parade, and then down Makeke Street.

Hark, it is time for the parade to begin. A screech of tires at the corner of Kaumauali'i and Ola and the parade has begun. This particular peacock is yellow with purple fenders and a red hood. You will note that the front tires are smaller than the rear tires and that every little bump makes the car bounce, as though something had happened to the suspension system. There is a pilot, who owns the car (or whose father owns the car) and also a co-pilot. To qualify the arms of both the pilot and the co-pilot must extend out of their respective windows and occasionally be raised in a 'shaka sign' when passing distinguished (young and beautiful) spectators.

The purpose of the co-pilot is to supply support. There must be a grin on his face as he surveys the crowd. He reports to the pilot telling him who is in the audience, as the pilot must keep his eyes on the road. His face shows that he is "proud as a peacock." In front of the viewing stand, which just happens to be the campus of the local high school, the chariot stops. The engine races and then with a screech, the tires spin and when there is sufficient smoke belching and rubber burning and smoking out of the rear of the car, it jerks ahead and we are

124

ready for contestant number two. Oh, did I forget to mention that there is something of a contestant factor in this parade?

This next contestant is a small Japanese model pickup truck. It is painted a rather bilgey shade of green, but the procedure is the same. Possibly there is just a little more screech of tires (if the pickup bed is empty and therefore does not have traction) before the car jumps ahead and all is well with contestant number two. Number three has an added attraction. Even before the corner is turned you can hear the throb of the woofers, a rumble similar to an earthquake but with a distinctive rhythm.

The antics of this car are similar. It is a red "push" so named because occasionally it takes one to get it started, but it is no relation to a Porsche. With the woofers and the tweeters, which are baby woofers, it is difficult to hear the engine roar, but roar it does. At the same place it is stopped and the same screechy start is made. The car bounces as it takes off, but the woofers and the tweeters don't miss a beat.

And so it continues, contestant after contestant, and then repeat after repeat, with boring regularity. They are good to each other and never are there two contestants in front of the viewing stand at the same time. Only occasionally does one find a dirt patch to dislocate with a spewing spray of rocks and dirt onto another contestant, which always leads to trouble as peacocks don't like to have their feathers ruffled.

The science of stopping and starting is highly developed. With left foot on the brake you accelerate to high revolutions per minute and then lift the left foot from the brake. This skill is gained through long hours of practice, always in front of the female grandstand and only when school officials and local constabulary officials are not in attendance.

Some peacocks are no longer in the running. They jerk up the hill, tires hardly worth the name, engines running roughly and the sound of iron filings grinding in the transmission. They have seen better days and there is little left for them but pasture. But the Peacock Parade continues year after year, with different contestants, different pilots and co-pilots; they call it more-of-the-same.

Truthfully we all like to strut. We don't all have the cars to pull off a parade, but we show it in our dressing, our actions and activities. We each want to be special, someone who makes a difference. We may do this through sports, cars, clothes, grades; you name it. But we want to be someone special.

Though not as loudly proclaimed, God does consider us as someone special. He deals with each of us in a unique way and that is what counts. I invite you to be a someone special by acknowledging him as God, and yourself as a child of God. No smoke, no woofers or tweeters, no burning rubber, no skid marks on the pavement, no dust spewed in someone else's face, just a very secure child of God.

That also means that we are humble about our relationship with God. No bragging about how great we are, how involved we are in his church, how many miracles we have managed to pull off, how many chapters of his Word we have memorized. As kids we need to show our parents that we are genuinely interested in the will of God, and as parents we need to show our kids that we are serious about our faith, not something once or twice a year, not a worship experience only when there is positively nothing else to do and it is a rainy day. We had better be genuine, and not a peacock, because God is genuine, to the nth degree.

"Gracious lord, keep me serious about my relationship with you. May your love guide my actions, my relationships with others and my goals and aims for my life. For I pray in your son's name. Amen."

LINDA

"When Jesus stepped ashore, he was met by a demon-possessed man from the town. For a long time this man had not worn clothes or lived in a house, but had lived in the tombs. When he saw Jesus, he cried out and fell at his feet, shouting at the top of his voice, 'What do you want with me, Jesus, Son of the Most High God. I beg you, don't torture me!' Jesus asked him, 'What is your name?' 'Legion,' he replied because many demons had gone into him. When the townspeople came to Jesus, they found the man from whom the demons had gone out, sitting at Jesus' feet, dressed and in his right mind; and, they were afraid. Those who had seen it told the people how the demon possessed man had been cured."

—Luke 8:27–28, 30, 36.

She appeared at the front door, a wild-eyed stare glazing her eyes. She had been found wandering around in the cemetery adjacent to the church and a kind teacher brought her to our front door. The teacher beat a hasty retreat, glad to have served, and gladder to have found someone with whom to leave her.

Though I welcomed her into the house, she was reluctant to enter, so we walked to the office a short block away. She seemed compelled to talk with very little time for listening. Her talking showed that she was disturbed. I struggled to get some kind of information out of her, to determine what she really wanted, as I was afraid that I knew what she needed. Her head had not seen a comb in recent days, though it appeared to be very lively, and her sole possession was a double plastic shopping bag ("Because I don't want others to be able to see what I have!") She was attracted to our church because it had an, "Old smell to it, like the smell of death, like my father's house." I had the distinct feeling that she would bolt at the slightest provocation so our conversation was light on the way to the office.

127

She had been, "Looking for the right Bible, the true Bible," and she would know it when she saw it. All of the other Bibles had been written by Hitler and she had the front half of the right Bible but had lost the last half. The True Bible ended with the words, in the book of Revelation, "The End." She would not come into the office, so we headed on to the Educational Center where we had five or six different kinds of Bibles. Of course none of them ended with, "The End." She was disturbed but not surprised. We were not the true church, so she had to go somewhere else. I offered her a place to sit and relax, or a place to stay overnight, but she would have none of it. I offered her a bag of food, but again she refused. She felt compelled to continue on in her search for the True Bible.

Her name was Linda, or at least that is what she said. She offered no last name and she did not know where she was from, nor know where she was going, and it seemed not to bother her at all. She would begin a sentence and then end some other sentence. Of course the truth was that she was serving a sentence of a troubled mind.

In several places in scripture there are stories of demoniacs living in the place of the dead (graveyard). They come out to where Jesus is and recognize him. He heals them and then sends the demons into a herd of pigs that is nearby. The pigs run to their destruction and the demoniacs live happily ever after. I have always been disturbed that they did not have names, as though the de-demonizing was more important than the fact that they were real people, born to someone, living in a home with someone and loved by someone.

I would love to say that Linda, last name unknown, was healed by her contact, brief though it was, with the church. But she did not come for healing, nor would she accept the healing much less anything else. She was on a crusade to find the 'right' Bible so that the Battle of Armagaddon would take place.

It is easy for me to say that she was a mental case, that proper psychological help, along with prescription drugs, would ease her troubled mind, heal her schizophrenia, or bi-polar problems. But who gave me the right to decide what was wrong with her and then prescribe something?

It would be easy for me to suggest that she had the wrong kind of theology, that somewhere some perverse theologian had implanted things in her mind and head that would disturb her without the counter-balance of God's love, a constant reassurance of peace through God.

It would have been easy for me to get her a place to stay, enough food to take care of her, training so that she would be a productive segment of society. We could have arranged for food stamps, county-assisted housing, and her needs would have been met, but she was on a different journey, one that would satisfy some deep theological urge, and I could not provide what she wanted.

We live in a world of Lindas. Oh, you won't run into one every day of your life, but they are all around you with needs like everyone else. If our health care system manages to catch up with a 'Linda' or she is taken care of, still the deep urge that she has is not met. Lindas are often happy in the places of the dead, for the folk there will listen and not talk back.

My prayer is that when you meet one, that you will be open to help where they want help. Christ always healed the obvious, though the healing was often on the way to the non-obvious. May we have the wisdom and power to do likewise.

"Loving Heavenly Father, it is as a humble child of God that we come to you about other children of yours. They have needs that we cannot satisfy, demands that we cannot meet, and problems to which we have no solutions. In your wisdom give us the power to give your love to all those whom we meet. If we cannot meet their needs then let us know, Father God, and help us to back off so that they can truly get the help that they need. In your son's name we pray. Amen."

GOLF CHICK

"Rich and poor have this in common: the Lord is the Maker of them all. The rich rule over the poor, the borrower is servant to the lender. A generous man will himself be blessed, for he shares his food with the poor. He who oppresses the poor to increase his wealth and he who gives gifts to the rich—both come to poverty."

—Proverbs 22:2,7,9,16.

As the clouds moved through the pass there would come periods of sunshine and then heavy mist, that could be considered rain. (We never bragged about the rain in Hawai'i, we would spend too much time bragging.) The rain did not deter those who were trying their skill at the miniature golf course. The Tee-off through the "St. Catherines Church" green was busy. Then you climbed up to the "Kileaua Light House" and then down to the "Slippery Slide" where the ball must be sliced through the "Lane of Trees" and "Sleeping Giant", until you came to "Mt. Wai'aleale" which necessitated slicing the ball straight up the valley or you would never find the cup. It was a good course that challenged you to not only play miniature golf but also become acquainted with beautiful Kaua'i.

It was a busy course. Two couples were spending more time with each other than the course. One tiny bride was receiving instruction from her husband and each lesson necessitated his putting his arms around her, which made it awkward, but fun. Another couple were studiously competing and were keeping track of each hole, when and where they made a hole-in-one and what was their running score.

Some junior high boys were playing the course as though it were a race. If they did not make a hole-in-one, it usually took either three or four shots and often the ball was guided in if it seemed that the next person in line was getting close. Twice they passed the couples but the couples seemed not to care. What bride and groom care about junior high boys in their way?

Adjacent to the miniature golf course was a hot dog stand and beyond that a tourist-trap, by the name of "The Tourist Trap". You could buy a hot dog or couples could buy an extra-long hot dog to share, mustard on his end and catchup on her's. Some hot dogs were spicier and hotter than others, and therefore called for a cold drink. All were fascinated watching the golfers.

Occasionally they would throw bits of the bun to the guinea fowl, peacocks and pigeons that had established themselves in what was to them a fast food outlet. In, around, above and adjacent to all were the usual Wild Jungle Fowl better known as wild chickens.

On the third round of golf that the junior high boys played, one came upon a small newly hatched chicken that was breathing its last. Jokingly they made as if to use it as a golf ball, but they were kind boys so they were no danger to the baby chick. Slowly it would wiggle its wings, never really getting on its feet or opening it's eyes. There was a certainty that early death was in its future.

Another boy decided that he would take it home to his mother (it was Mothers' Day) and so picked it up and began inquiring about what it should be fed. Milk did not seem to be the best thing but barn-yard knowledge was scarce at that point. Then he noticed that the chick had lice and it was soon left resting next to the "Sleeping Giant Hole" while the boy went to wash up. All thoughts of compassion were gone and soon the boys were, too. So there the little chick passed away, died, went pau. A source of food was nearby, it had great need, but the food and the starving one could not be put together.

One of the great deterrents to benevolence in the world today is that the recipients, those who are starving, those who have great need, have lice. They are really very unpleasant people. Often they are dirty, they are smelly, all they think about is food, and rather than being thankful, with long letters of appreciation, all they do is eat everything that you give them and come up asking for more. They always seem to agree with your political system. Somehow their political beliefs or views are only determined by who gives them food. They are politically wishy-washy, depending upon the source of food or aid.

If the sun is out, they are hot. If the sun is not out, they are cold. If it is raining, they are wet. They never seem to be able to take care of themselves. And they are always invisibly visible. If you wish to see them, they are there. If you do not wish to see them, then they are not there.

Christ's words indicate that we are to find the poor and needy. They do not have the responsibility to find us. We are not our brother's keeper, but we are his sharer! If they have lice, so be it. They are hungry and in need. There is a gulf between them and us and it is up to us to bridge it.

You don't need to be thanked for sharing bread. You don't need to make a mission trip in order to see for yourself that they are hungry. (Possibly the money spent on the mission trip could better be used to feed the hungry.) They do not enjoy being stared at, though that is the only way that they can get enough to fill their stomachs. There are many agencies and there are way more needs than the agencies tell us about. You may not get IRS credit for giving to the needy, you may never get your name on a brochure that you can show to your friends, but God knows where is the need and where are the resources. Consider yourself a bridge. The only permission we need to fill their food needs is their appetite. Bon appetit.

"Gracious Lord, give us the grace to fill the needs of those who are greatly in need. May our willingness outshine their need, that we might be brothers and sisters on the earth with you as our heavenly father. In your son's name we pray. Amen."

WILD JUNGLE FOWL

"O Jerusalem, Jerusalem, you who kill the prophets and stone those sent to you, how often I have longed to gather your children together, as a hen gathers her chicks under her wings, but you were not willing. Look! Your house is left to you desolate. For I tell you, you will not see me again until you say, 'Blessed is he who comes in the name of the Lord.'"

—Matthew 23, 37–39

Come to my house and here we can watch greed, passion, anger, sex, frustration, concern, fear, hate, rejection, family love, and just about every other emotion in the book. You sit over there and let's talk about our neighbors, the Wild Jungle Fowl. I would love to name them but they are wild and besides if you name someone or something then you become attached to them or it, and I must confess that to them I am attached. Therefore let me name them.

King of the yard is George, a beautiful bantam rooster who not only looks kingly but struts with all the authority of his being. He has beaten back pretenders to the throne but he reins supreme. Though he spends much time protecting his turf, which he thinks that my lawn is, his crowing is an articulate call to his mate who is Henryetta. She is a spotted hen and gladly joins George in ruling the lawn. The pretender to the throne is Francis, a totally black rooster but no match for George.

There are another fifteen or sixteen consisting of mostly hens but one rooster who was very sickly and weak but has developed into a possible contender for the throne presently occupied by George. The enemy that they all face are the three or four feral cats that also inhabit the lawn, staying mostly at the edge brush. They will not attack the group as long as George is present.

We do regularly feed the Wild Jungle Fowl. They need to be kept wild in order to protect themselves and that means finding their own food, even if they have to dig up our lawn to find it. We do feed wild birds, occasionally. The reason for the "occasionally" is that they also need to keep up their hunt for wild seeds and to feed them too often makes them dependent upon you. But the bird

133

feeder that we maintain is made for small birds and the chickens and roosters and even the doves and mynah birds can not fit on it. However the small birds are messy in their eagerness to eat the seeds so the seeds spill onto the ground and therefore are intended for the Wild Jungle Fowl.

In a way the Wild Jungle Fowl have adopted us. They manage to scrounge around all the flower beds, and even the lawn digging for bugs, seeds or whatever, so that mowing the lawn is difficult because of the holes. For a while George was minus his tail feathers. They were lost in a defense of his family from a large neighborhood dog. The ultimate defense was to let the dog grab his tail feathers and then wiggle loose, for by that time his hen and chicks had escaped and he went from a loss of tail feathers to full flight and landed about a hundred feet away. He looked strange for a while, sort of a combination of rooster in front and hen behind, but we are proud of his fighting abilities and I have not heard any other rooster brag about their feathers. Henryetta with her chicks roosts in the nearby bougainvilla tree and George stands guard on some of the lower branches.

Wild Jungle Fowl are very family oriented. They have gone through the loss of eight chicks and it seems to have been a painful experience. No doubt they will try to replace them. The remaining chicks seem old enough we expect another batch any day now.

Francis has a hen that is speckled with white spots all over her. Just what her genetic history is, of course we do not know. She has one chick left of her brood, now a teenager, and she is mottled tan. The chick sticks close to her mother, so close that often she precedes the mother hen. The rooster always accompanies his family and when there are seeds, or anything else available for food he calls her and she comes running. Of course the other chickens do, also. The rooster has been known, many times, to drive all other chickens, mynah birds and also doves away until his hen is finished eating along with her tan offspring. They nest just over the wall at the back of our lawn and even show signs of loyalty whenever I leave the house with my large hat on. I imagine that I have been scolded often but then I don't understand chicken talk so I don't really know that. It is true, though, that he responds to me often and to my wife seldom. If I bring the bird feeder into the house to refill it he hangs around and is totally unafraid of me.

I find that the chickens are very loyal to me. When I mow the lawn they follow closely. Of course the fact that the mower stirs up bugs could not be the reason for their loyalty.

Being in our yard is not necessarily a safe place to be but the lawn is large enough that any cat, of which we have two feral, has a long way to go to the bird feeder, which gives any alert rooster and his family ample warning to scoot.

We often have dogs that wander through the yard but they are no match for our chickens. We have had a wild pig but he seemed to have nothing to do with our Wild Jungle Fowl. Wild Jungle Fowl fly, often and fast and far. The kiawe tree at the front of the yard houses both feral cats and also chickens. The chickens are so far out on the branches that the cats can't get to them but there the chickens can keep their eye, or is it eyes, on the opposition.

Seldom do the cats attack a family. Those spikes located on the backs of the legs of the roosters are a great deterrent. I neglected to mention there is one lone chicken, who seems to like it that way. She is not part of any family, nor does she want to become part of a family. She is likewise chased away from the choice bits of food that might be found but she does keep herself trim and in good flying condition.

Sitting in the back yard, one can experience just about every emotion that the Wild Jungle Fowl display. These are not barnyard chickens. They are free, independent and are fiercely loyal to each other. Whether I leave or arrive home during the daylight George is always there to greet me. George will come up to me and talk in his low rumbling cackle. The only thing that keeps us from communicating is that I do not understand him. I can figure out what he wants, though, and he keeps his eye on me. Of course with the other eye he is on the watch for the cats.

But the pleasant surprise is to surprise the hen, with her rooster close by, and when she moves off to see the chicks that she has been sheltering, follow her. This was the maternal-paternal feeling that Jesus had when he expressed his love for his followers. This love and affection also exists between the pastor and the flock whom God has called him or her to serve. Little do the church members know of the warm care or feeling that the pastor has for the congregation, the disappointment that exists when some one of the flock moves off to either another leader or to inextricable trouble. There is joy at the success of the members of the congregation. So, every time that any of the disciples saw a chicken and her small brood they would be reminded that Jesus had the same feelings for those he came to save. True pastors have the same feelings for their flock, and indeed that is why they are considered a flock.

We take the Wild Jungle Fowl-chicken situation for granted here in Hawai'i, and only when someone calls from the mainland and almost immediately says, "Are those chickens I hear in the background?" do we realize that we also take for granted the affectionate relationships that pastors have for congregations and also the affectionate relationship and regard that Jesus Christ has for human beings. The crowing of the roosters, the cackle of the hens is so much a part of our lives that we hardly notice their presence.

Could it be that our relationship with God is also so taken for granted we do not recognize the many blessings that are contained, not just in our back yards but throughout our lives.

"Gracious heavenly Father, keep us aware of your love for us. It begins with our being, and then continues on through our lives as we insert ourselves into your will. It will continue on into and through eternity as we move into that relationship with you. May we always be aware of that love and always be a credit to you so that we were not created in vain, but rather to be close to you and your love. In your son's name we pray. Amen."

THE GROCERY BAG

"My righteousness draws near speedily, my salvation is on the way, and my arm will bring justice to the nations. The islands will look to me and wait in hope for my arm. Lift up your eyes to the heavens, look at the earth beneath; the heavens will vanish like smoke, the earth will wear out like a garment and its inhabitants die like flies. But my salvation will last forever, my righteousness will never fail."

—Isaiah 51:5,6

His early life in Japan was simple. With his three brothers, mother and father, he lived in a house, consisting of one long room, which served all the purposes that we now incorporate into our multi-room and multi-level homes. Water was provided by a bamboo pipe that brought the water in from a neighboring stream to a centralized tub. When the tub was filled, another bamboo pipe took the excess back to the stream. The family owned only necessities for daily living and they were used regularly each day of the week.

At night time, when the duties of the day were over, the futons came off the shelf and the room became a large sleeping area. In the morning the futons went back on the shelf and life proceeded. HS was born May 14th, 1900, in Soneda, in the state of Fukuoka in Japan, and was named Saburo, which means third son.

His father's name was Fukujiro Shinagawa; the Jiro meant that he was the second son, with almost no inheritance. So he was adopted into the Kawakami family where he was treated as a first son, the head of the family. He was a large, well liked man.

Soneda was a farming community that raised rice, wheat and lots of vegetables, but HS early decided not to become a farmer. He had inherited an excitement for fun and games from his father, and the desire to be wealthy. From his mother he inherited his slight size and a propensity for seasickness.

In 1912, HS in a seasick haze, sailed with a friend to Honolulu. There he went through immigration with a tag that read, "Saburo Kawakami, destination Port Allen (Kaua'i)" so that he would not be lost in transit. When he arrived in Port

Allen, the seaport for the Island of Kaua'i, he was met by the part of the family that had preceded him, and immediately was enrolled in school where the major study was English. Soon he was enrolled in Mid-Pacific Institute in Honolulu. Mid-Pacific was the combination of many missionary schools and catered mainly to Japanese students.

HS was thirteen when he enrolled in third grade and larger than most of the boys in his class. Classes were held from Tuesday through Saturday and, though it was tempting to speak Japanese their purpose for being there was to learn English. Saburo decided that he should have an English name so he became Henry Saburo soon shortened to HS. At Mid-Pac he learned the saying, "Sweet are the uses of adversity..." from The Merchant of Venice. He would quote it often during his life as he faced adversity.

Mid-Pac also had a work program so HS worked in a pineapple factory, a sugar cane factory on Kaua'i and in a flower shop in Honolulu. It was in the flower shop that he experienced working in a family business relationship, and he liked it. He wanted to be in commercial work and when he graduated from Mid-Pac, it was said that he would be, "such an honest and hard-working man." Considering himself behind in his life plan, he determined he would not continue on to college but rather would enter the work force.

Because of his ability at sports HS was offered a job with a sugar company in Makaweli on Kaua'i and was involved in accounting and inventory. He worked hard but felt that there was discrimination on the plantation, and therefore planned to leave its employment. A friend, knowing that he was contemplating the move gave him three pieces of advice: 1. Even if you have to be independent, it is better to carry two baskets on your shoulder. (Be the employer and also the employee) 2. You have to take care of your health. 3. A small crack in the dam can damage the whole reservoir, (pay attention to the small things).

Throughout his life, business, social or other professional relationships, HS would be alert to the problem of prejudice and would actively work against it, alert to the needs of the individual as against the possible prejudice of the organization. If there were business clubs, he would choose the one with the haoles (foreigners, English speaking) in it. If there was a choice in any of the professional groups that he would be associated with, he likewise chose that group that had haoles in its membership.

As an independent worker he struggled and met each adversity as it arose. He worked through all the positions in a local grocery store, making changes as he felt necessary. Home deliveries were a regular part of the grocer's life. He would go out in the community to take orders in the morning and back out in the afternoon to fill them for his customers. Few had cars that could be used for shopping. Therefore he carried thousands of bags of groceries for his customers.

The store that he established was the first of many stores on the Island of Kaua'i. He required all of his employees to put the customer first, without exception. Everyone was welcomed to his store, everyone was served and everyone was happy. Finally the resulting company was "Big Save", what is now the western-most grocery chain in the world, located on the Island of Kaua'i. In his retirement years he would still be active in the local Waimea store and would bag groceries and carry them to the customers' cars. He was still concerned with individuals.

It was in that store and at that checkout counter where HS had bagged groceries many years before, that a customer came with a cloth grocery bag. The checkout cashier could not fathom what she was supposed to do, for she had always bagged groceries in the plastic bags. She put the groceries in plastic then in the cloth bag but was aware of the fact that she didn't need the plastic. Possibly it was the turning point in American society. Cloth bags had been the only kind used in HS's first grocery days.

Cloth, reusable bags, are used by just about every country in the world, except the U. S. A. Cloth bags carry more groceries than plastic, are stronger, and have web handles so that there is less strain on the fingers of the hand. Being cloth they can't be overloaded, will not tear and spill the contents on the feet of the handler. Cloth bags are used over and over, and are not blowing through the air, until caught in trees or tumbling along the beaches where they are air borne until water borne, like the plastic bags found in almost all American Stores.

After a while, on the Island of Kaua'i, you could tell where the plastic bags came from by the color, whether white with green letters, white with red letters, yellow with red letters, blue green or whatever. Plastic grocery bags are made from petroleum products, and are seldom used more than once.

As for cloth grocery bags, there are blanks, that is bags with no printing on them, found in many stores that can be dyed any color you wish. Or the bags can be made out of material by volunteer groups, church groups, service clubs, sports activity groups, possibly sold for cost.

Blanks, on which you can put your own printing, can be purchased from Bag Works in Forth Worth, TX, or ordered on the internet at Http:www. bagworks.com. Wal-mart, Target, K Mart and ACE Hardware all stock them. Cloth bags are sold by the United States Postal Service with many different logos or designs, some commemorating stamps and others commemorating particular service organizations or subjects. Every zip code has them.

Instead of advertising the store on disposable plastic that is hardly noticed, stores could sell bags with their own logos on them. But more than the logos that they may carry, they do advertise that we as a nation and the concerned people within it, need to conserve all the nonrenewable resources that we have, and that the holder of the bag is doing his or her part to use reusable materials.

Again the saying that HS memorized from his days at Mid-Pacific comes to mind, "Sweet are the uses of adversity." In a world that is facing the expending of its natural resources at an alarming rate, the use of cloth grocery bags reminds us of other ways to conserve God's gift of what we enjoy in today's life. HS enjoyed serving his community, the town of Waimea, the Island of Kaua'i and the state of Hawai'i. Through his store, through his church and through his service club he was aware of the needs of the world.

1. To save electricity: conversion to florescent bulbs from incandescent, turning off the lights that you are not using, turning down the heat in the summer time, the use of wind for air cooling homes, supporting of a wind power program of your local utility, when showering wet, turn off the water when you lather and then wash.

2. To save petroleum: along with the use of cloth grocery bags, urge the use of gasohol, driving below the speed limit, stop drag racing from one stop light to another, walking for local trips and shopping through your fingers walking the yellow section of your telephone book.

3. Generally: use of Sunday comic section for wrapping paper for holidays, for a year, at least, wear clothes that you already have in your closet, pick up all trash and recycle what is recyclable, use vegetables as garden plants, they are beautiful as well as delicious, insist on smaller portions in restaurants, use a home purifier rather than purchasing bottled water, take time to smell and see the flowers.

4. Be inventive: share your conservation secrets with your neighbors, family and friends. Use the rummage and garage sales for necessary purchases, list things that each member of your family can do to be conservative in your life style. Make conservation fun for yourself and for the entire family.

HS was a plain but determined man. He worked hard all his life and was always aware of the individuals with whom he did business. He knew just about everyone in his area of the Island of Kaua'i and he was openly happy to greet each individual. He wanted his family to remain together and so he promoted family associations.

We, as citizens of the one world need to realize that God has made us as brothers and sisters in the physical world that he has created. His desire is that we cooperate in keeping the resources intact, that together we might honor and glorify Him, both now and in the future He has planned for us. Isaiah's prophecy is very pertinent to our age, and indeed to every age.

"Gracious Father, we appreciate the world of which we are a part. We pray that all mankind might experience and appreciate the blessings that we have. Help us to live our lives aware, not only of others around us but, also of future generations, that we might conserve what we have and pass on not only the land but also the awareness of you and your love. In your Son's name we pray. Amen"

EPILOGUE

To you the reader:

I hope that you have had as much fun reading as I have had writing, and recollecting these parables. After the proof reader has gone through them several times, and then I have gone through them again several times and then the illustrator has gone through them, the various incidents and conversations stand out as very real parabolic encounters. Each parable could well be made into a twenty minute sermon.

I have often been asked, "What is your theology?" It would be possible for me to write a theological book but I am reminded that Jesus did not do that but rather told parables that explained his theology. I am aware that the parables here partially explain my theology.

Most of the differing theological discussions of today are not based on the Gospels, the words and works of Jesus, but rather on other Biblical sources. Though of course there is much straight forward theology in Christ's teachings the parables are easily understood by persons of different cultural backgrounds, by those of intellectual mind and also the kindergarten drop-outs, by those who are economically well to do and also by those who pulled the book out of the dumpster and read it sitting on a building exhaust vent to keep warm along with several layers of newspapers insulating their body, with a street light as their source of light.

I urge you to see the parables that are around you. Daily we see persons, incidents or have experiences that reveal God's love and his will for our lives. I urge you to share your own parables with others that our bank-of-faith-knowledge might continually have deposits.

I also urge you to consider strongly the title parable, <u>The Grocery Bag</u>, in your daily living. You no doubt have many concepts about living conservatively in our present age. Share those concepts with others. Christ's political movement was to change the individual who would in turn change society, physically and spiritually.

143

A hui hou aku   **(until we meet again)**

SCRIPTURE REFERENCE

GLOSSARY OF HAWAIIAN WORDS

'AINA	Land, earth, country.
ALOHA	Love, loved one. The most used word in Hawai'i.
HAOLE	A white person. A foreigner who was brought to the Island of Hawai'i. The white person might have been born in Hawaii, but was still haole.
HO'OPONOPONO	To correct or revise or make a mental or spiritual cleansing of the family by family discussion and prayer.
HULA	The native song, chant, dance of the islands. The dance tells a story expressed by body movements.
KAMA'AINA	Native born, (land child), native plant.
KEIKI	Child, descendant, offspring. To become a child.
LANAI	A porch or veranda of a small building near a house or home.
LEI	A garland, wreath or necklace of flowers shells ivory beads and sometimes dollar bills, worn around the neck.
MAKAI	Toward the ocean. Because Hawai'i is composed of islands, direction is often given with "Makai" toward the ocean or "Mauka" toward the mountains. Other directions are given toward a large town in either direction.
MALAHINI	A newcomer to the islands or a stranger among others who know each other well.
MAUKA	Toward the mountains. See makai, above.
MENEHUNES	Legendary race of small people who worked at night building roads, fish ponds, temples. If the work was not finished in one night it was left unfinished.
'OHANA	Family, group of relatives. Sometimes loosely defined. Also to gather together for family prayer.
PALI	A cliff or a very steep place.

PAU	Something completely finished, ended. Possibly the most used Hawaiian word in the language.
PAU HANA	End of work, quitting time. Often a time to gather for 'talk story' before heading home for the day
POI	The Hawaiian staff of life made from cooked taro corms, pounded or blended until smooth. No Hawaiian meal is complete without poi.
PUKA	A hole. Referred also to a door or an opening. Made famous by the stringing of shells that have pukas.
SHAKA	There are no Hawaiian words that begin with the letter "S". But the shaka sign consists of the thumb and little finger extended and the middle three fingers held in a clasp. Usually extended out to a friend or possibly a contender.
TUTU	There are no Hawaiian words, presently beginning with the letter "T". Ancient Hawaiian did include words that used the initial "T" for the letter "K" Tutu, then would be Kuku, or grandmother, particularly if wahini (woman) was used as a modifier.

978-0-595-37635-3
0-595-37635-5

Printed in the United States
39739LVS00005BA/394-441

9 780595 376353